Classic
INDIAN
C·U·I·S·I·N·E

Edited by Rosemary Moon

SMITHMARK

ILLUSTRATIONS BY
CAMILLA SOPWITH AND SALLY BREWER

CLB 4366
© 1995 CLB Publishing

This edition published in 1995 by Smithmark Publishers, Inc.
16 East 32nd Street, New York NY 10016

SMITHMARK books are available for bulk purchase for sales promotion
and premium use. For details write or call the manager of special sales,
SMITHMARK Publishers, Inc.
16 East 32nd Street, New York,
NY 10016; (212) 532-6600

Produced by CLB Publishing
Godalming Business Centre
Woolsack Way, Godalming, Surrey, UK

ISBN 0-8317-1177-9

Printed in South Africa
10 9 8 7 6 5 4 3 2 1

Contents

INTRODUCTION

Indian cuisine justifiably ranks amongst the finest in the world. It is a fascinating amalgamation of the practises of many different cultures and religions, the best of each having been absorbed into the classic dishes of this great sub-continent.

Indian Cooking in the West

There is no doubt at all that there is a great deal of interest in the west in Indian cooking. In the United States there is a growing number of Indian restaurants, especially on the east and west coasts where there are substantial populations of Indian immigrants. They are most likely to be found in the larger, more cosmopolitan cities. Such is the interest in Indian food that it is becoming a popular alternative style of home cooking, not just for young people but for those of all ages. It is especially popular – and please do forgive this slightly sexist remark – with men who are weekend hobby-cooks and really enjoy a day dabbling in the kitchen.

Indian restaurants are, however, less common in the United States than Mexican and Chinese ones – there are Mexican restaurants in almost every main street. It is interesting to note that though Chinese food has adapted quite dramatically to suit the tastes of westerners, Indian food has arrived making far fewer concessions to our preconceived ideas relating to food and culinary traditions. Probably the biggest change is the inclusion of appetizers in the typical Indian restaurant menu – such a concept of courses within a meal is virtually unknown to the majority of Indians. The more cosmopolitan communities in India have now adopted this western style of eating, previously only followed for banquets and celebratory meals.

The one slightly misleading impression that a western restaurant may give of classic Indian cooking is that it often features mushrooms. They are actually a fairly uncommon vegetable in India and are grown mainly in the far north, so the mushroom is not really a classic Indian ingredient.

Sensible Shopping

With the increasing interest in Indian cooking there have been many new products introduced in our stores in the way of sauces, pickles, relishes and spice blends for various styles of cooking. My advice when selecting such items is to pick those made by an Indian company if possible, rather than by a multi-national. The flavors and textures will be far more authentic and there are likely to be fewer additional cereal thickening agents – many classic Indian dishes are actually thickened by the use of puréed vegetables such as onions, giving a more intense and brighter flavor to the dish than would be achieved with cornstarch or any other cereal thickener.

I, in common with many other avid curry cooks, will travel miles out of my way to find my favorite curry pastes, pickles and relishes. They are such a basic, integral part of successful Indian cooking that the store-cupboard can never contain too large a selection. In many parts of the States you will have to visit specialist Indian shops for some of the ingredients in the recipes included in this book. Make the most of the opportunity to stock up on the goods they offer.

The World's Great Religions

There are communities in India that follow just about all the great religions of the world, and each contributes to the classic cuisine of the country, through its customs and beliefs. While many religions flourish in India there are two that dominate the country now, as they have throughout history. The followers of these religions are the Hindus and the Muslims.

The Sacred Cow

The majority of Indians are Hindus and they do not eat beef or veal, as they regard the cow as sacred. This reverence is said to extend back to the start of civilization as we know it, right back to the earliest farmers who decided that the nomadic life was not for them and that they would settle in one place. These first settlements were in the great river valleys of the Middle East and soon, as people began to want a patch of their own, the settlements spread as far as the Danube, across into China and down through Iran into India.

The early settlers grew crops and grazed cattle, one of the first animals to be domesticated. The cattle were kept for milk, meat and leather. However, an expanding population meant that the cattle were soon in short supply and they were eventually kept more for their milk than for their meat. Once the Hindu religion was established the cow was regarded as sacred and was no longer eaten – this must have been one of the very earliest examples of a successful conservation project.

The Muslim Influence

The Moguls, a Muslim people, invaded India from central Asia in the sixteenth century, bringing with them many culinary customs including the halal kill, a method of slaughtering meat, and the tradition of never eating pork, which is regarded as unclean. Considering that these people came from central Asia it is difficult to understand the ban on pork. It is widely eaten throughout the continent and features strongly in the cuisine of many of India's neighbouring countries. Muslims meat dishes are based on sheep, goats and chicken.

It seems to me that the Muslim people are particularly good cooks. Their influence is strongest in northern India, where meat cooking is at its best and the food tends to be richer, cooked in plenty of ghee or butter.

The Pork Dishes of the Goan Christians

There is pork in India – the Christian communities established in the times of the Portuguese settlers on the west coast around Goa have developed some classic pork curries containing coconut, mangoes and other local produce. This is really the only part of India where pig farming is carried out as, foragers that they are, pigs are not suited to life in desert conditions.

When the British were established in India in the days of the Raj there was a fair exchange of ideas about cooking. One of the most famous dishes to emerge from around this time is kedgeree, said to have been made by the Scottish community in India who were pining for their beloved smoked haddock. Kedgeree is a mixture of smoked haddock, rice, hard-boiled eggs, onions and curry paste or spices. The curry paste is omitted by many people in the west but, to me, the dish is incomplete without it. Kedgeree is more usually served as a lunch or supper dish but it is also delicious at breakfast time – although I can understand leaving the spices out at that time of day!

Afternoon Tea

During the days of the Raj another English custom became well established amongst parts of the Indian community – that of afternoon tea and freshly cut sandwiches. This may sound rather bizarre amongst the traditional perception of classic Indian cuisine, and there are no sandwich recipes contained in this book although banana sandwiches, perhaps developed in India, are one of my favorites! I have read an article by an established Indian food writer who is most grateful to the English for the introduction of the white loaf – a food that I would regard as a mixed blessing. Afternoon tea is very popular in India to this day amongst the professional people in larger cities.

Parsee Traditions from Persia

One of my favorite styles of Indian cooking is that of the Parsees, a tribe who came to India from Persia and settled in Bombay and the neighbouring area of Gujarat. I find their food to be rich and complex in flavor, with subtle but imaginative use of fruits such as apricots. A typical Parsee garnish for meat dishes is deep-fried potato straws, which provide a crisp contrast to the curries with which they are served.

Convenience Foods and Restaurants

When India gained its Independence in 1947 life began to change, especially in the cities and towns. Industrial and economic expansion meant that more women worked and there was less time to prepare many of the spices and relishes that had traditionally been made in the home. Ghee, a clarified butter, had always been made at home and even the wheat for chapatis was ground into fine flour in each household using a chakki, two heavy millstones on top of each other.

The middle classes had always had domestic help and so many of the more tedious kitchen tasks would have been carried out by the staff. To a great extent this is now a way of life belonging to the past – most people live in flats without servants and there is simply not the room for the equipment required to carry on as before, or the time to undertake so much home processing of basic ingredients. So prepared relishes, cooking fats and flour are now more widely available and commonly used than ever before, but the basic skills of the Indian cook remain superb.

Home Cooking is Best

Despite the proliferation of Indian restaurants in the west it is interesting to note that very few families go to restaurants in India even now. It is a land of home cooking, where pride is taken in the preparation of food for friends and family and where the restaurants would have great difficulty in competing with the skills of even the average home cook. It is a privilege to be invited to an Indian home for a meal, an experience to be savored. I have never had that pleasure but my father, who has visited India several times, has enjoyed a meal with colleagues in their home and talks about it at length! Nothing is too much trouble for an Indian family when they are entertaining – they have a marvellous culinary tradition to share with you, bound up in a more than generous hospitality, and they go out of their way to make every mouthful as enjoyable as possible.

Eating an Indian Meal

There are many customs that are changing in India and, in such a large country where there are the very rich and the exceptionally poor, it is difficult to say how a meal is most frequently served. Doubtless the middle classes and the vast majority of people living in the comfortable suburbs now eat using cutlery and china plates. However, this is something new, and the traditional way of eating, still followed by the vast majority, is with the fingers and from a banana leaf which acts as a plate.

Meals are most commonly eaten in the kitchen – dining rooms are a very unusual feature in an Indian home. There is a ritual of hand and feet washing before a meal is begun and shoes are never worn in the kitchen. The food is very often prepared by the cook as he or she sits on the floor and the floor must therefore be kept as clean as possible, thus shoes are banned. However, time brings changes and some families now eat at a table in the kitchen and occasionally use a spoon to gather up any remaining food from their banana leaves or plates. The vast majority of Indians do still eat with their fingers, which is why breads are such an important feature in an Indian meal, being used as scoops for the food.

It is second nature for Indians to wash their hands after a meal as well as before, to remove any stickiness from the food which has been eaten with the fingers. It is said that the tradition of rinsing the mouth after eating is responsible for the lack of dental treatment required by the average Indian during his or her lifetime.

A Tradition of Home Baking

I meet so many people who say that they would like to make their own bread but that they simply do not have the time to do so. Well, that may be the case in the west, where bread is either raised with yeast or naturally fermented from a sourdough, but in India most breads are made at home and are quick both to prepare and to cook. This is because the vast majority of them are unleavened, and are simply mixed and then baked.

The easiest and quickest Indian bread must be the chapati. These are mixed, left for 30 minutes and then rolled out and cooked on a griddle or in a dry skillet for about four minutes. The first time that we made them, my husband (who is really the bread maker in our house) was convinced that they were going to taste like cardboard but they were delicious! Please do follow the recipe in this book and make a little foil package to keep the finished chapatis warm while the others are cooking.

13

It really is simple!

Breads were traditionally made by the ladies of the household and, as they are at their best when freshly cooked immediately before a meal, it became quite natural for the women to eat after everyone else, once they had finished the cooking.

When making a leavened Indian bread it is very easy for us to cover the dough and place it in a warm place to rise, but the average Indian would not have a suitable warm place. The traditional Indian way of speeding the proofing of the dough would be to warm a metal bowl with hot water, drain it and dry it and then to place the dough in the warmed bowl to rise – it is a simple method that works well.

The very finely ground flours that are used for making Indian breads are available in the west in healthfood shops and specialist Indian shops. It is difficult to get really good results without the correct flour but I have made reasonable chapatis using fine whole wheat flour – traditional western whole wheat bread-making flour is far too coarse to give good results. It is interesting to note that although many of the Indian breads that are now sold in western supermarkets are made with white flour, the traditional Indian bread flour is whole wheat, although it is so finely ground that it is very pale in color.

A Rice Toddy

There is a most unusual bread that is made in the south of India – there is no recipe for it in this book as it would be difficult to get the ingredients but the description of it is most interesting. It is made with a rice flour, finely ground for bread making, and is leavened with toddy, not a restorative alcoholic drink but the fermented juice of the coconut palm.

Rice – a Staple Food Synonymous with Curry

Although in the west we tend to assume that curry and rice are always served together, this simply is not true. Some Indians are great rice eaters and it is their staple food, but there are many others who eat mainly bread and seldom have rice. It all depends on where they live. Roughly speaking, wheat is more widely grown in the north and west of India and these are the areas where bread is the staple food of the majority of people. Rice is grown throughout the south and in the central and northern river valleys. The city of Patna on the River Ganges in the north east of India is synonymous with rice the world over.

Around half of the world's population eat rice as their staple food and India is the second largest grower, producing 19 per cent of the world's total crop. Rice needs moist, temperate conditions in which to grow and the rice fields, usually known as paddy fields, may be artificially flooded to provide the right conditions if they are not naturally moist enough. There are a few varieties of upland rice which grow well in drier conditions but these are not so common. The sowing and harvesting of rice has traditionally been done by hand, by workers standing in the flooded fields to sow the seeds or to plant out the seedlings. They later wade through the ripe crop, picking the husks of rice which resemble mature oats when ready for harvest. Seed is now sometimes sown from low-flying aircraft.

To Process or not to Process

Grains of rice come well packaged! They are contained within an outer layer of husk which, when removed, reveals the protective bran. The rice at this stage is what we call brown rice and many people like to eat the rice with the bran which provides extra roughage in the diet. Care should be taken when cooking brown rice – never add salt to the water or use a salted stock as this will toughen the bran and the grain, retarding cooking and making it somewhat akin to a miniature bullet! The vast majority of rice is polished before it is packaged for the market. The polishing removes the bran and produces the white grains with which we are all familiar.

Basmati Rice – the Best

Basmati rice is actually native to Pakistan, which borders the north west of India, but the fine, long-grain rice with a delicate flavor is the most popular for Indian cooking. The slogan to be found on many basmati rice packages proclaims that the grains are washed by the waters of the Himalayas – this certainly produces excellent rice.

Wash it Well

Many rices are pre-washed in the west and, although such treatment ensures that they cook well with separate grains, it does reduce the flavor of the rice because of the extra processing. I prefer to buy white rice, preferably basmati, and to wash it myself, removing all the excess starch from the grains and thus ensuring a good cooked result.

Other tips for cooking rice are given in the introduction to the rice recipes. However, one of my favorite ways of preparing it is not featured in this book so I will describe it here briefly. It is a method for cooking rice in the oven and is especially good when entertaining as it can just be left to its own devices.

This method is often used in Indian restaurants as the rice may be prepared and left for an hour or more without coming to any harm. You need a very large baking dish, suitable for use on the hob and in the oven, that will allow the rice to boil without boiling over. It should have a tight-fitting lid but I have found that the rice cooks best if a stainless steel or enamel dish is used. Cast iron would seem to be a natural choice but, in my experience, it retains the heat so well that the rice tends to stick and dry out around the sides of the dish. A good tip if using cast iron is to leave the rice in the oven for no longer than one hour.

Always use basmati rice and wash it well. Use 1½ cups rice to 2½ cups liquid for the actual cooking of the rice. The rice should be weighed dry and then left to soak in water for at least 30 minutes. Drain the soaked rice in a strainer and discard the water. Bring the measured liquid to a boil in a separate pan – use water or a mixture of milk and water for a more flavorsome rice. Heat 1 tablespoon of ghee or sweet butter in the baking dish and fry a selection of spices, including bay leaves and a cinnamon stick, for 30 seconds, then add the rice and fry it until it is coated with the ghee and hot. Stir in the boiled liquid and return it quickly to a boil, cover and leave well alone over medium to high heat for 8 minutes, ensuring that the rice does not boil over.

Look at the rice after 8 minutes – the liquid should have disappeared from the top of the pan, leaving the surface of the rice fully exposed. If this is not so, cover the pan again and cook for a further minute or two. Stir the rice briefly to ensure that it has not stuck to the base of the pan, then cover the dish again and place it in the oven at its lowest temperature. Leave it alone for at least one hour and you will have perfect rice. The timing of the boiling, ensuring that all the liquid is gone from the surface of the rice before it is transferred to the oven, is the secret of success with this method of rice cookery.

The Art of the Masala

Masala is a word that keeps turning up in Indian culinary terminology. It is often used to describe a curry of medium heat but is actually defined as a combination of spices, or spices and herbs. A masala is therefore an essential part of almost every Indian dish (with the exception of some sweet ones) and it may be mild or so strong that it will make your eyes water! The blending of masalas indicates the skill of the cook. Garam masala is a mix of curry spices used as a basis for many dishes – it lacks much of the floury taste of some curry powders (a virtually unknown ingredient in India) and may be used as a garnish, added to a dish at the last moment. This is a store-cupboard essential for the avid curry cook.

The Skill of Spicing

Westerners have a reputation for under-seasoning their food, preferring it to be bland and somewhat dull. Well, if you are keen on Indian food that obviously is not an accurate description of your tastes! However, in order to achieve a good variety of flavors in your masalas and to really enjoy cooking authentic Indian food it is essential to have a good selection of spices in your store cupboard and to experiment with them to discover their flavors.

Buying for Freshness

Once spices have been ground they start to deteriorate, so it is preferable either to grind them as you need them, or to buy them ready ground in small quantities which you use up quickly while the flavors are at their best. I would say that three months is the optimum storage time for ground spices, and that after six months they will be well on the way to staleness. Spice racks look very pretty on the kitchen wall but they do the spices stored in them no good at all. Spices are best kept in air-tight containers in a dark cupboard or drawer. I store most of mine in special containers with divided tops, allowing the spices to be shaken out or measured by the teaspoon, but I still keep the pots in a drawer.

Buying spices in small quantities will not necessarily ensure that they are fresh if you buy them from a small store. I would therefore suggest that you buy date-stamped bottles or jars, an expensive way of purchasing but you will at least have a guide to when the spices should be at their best. A cheaper way of buying, and the best way for a keen cook, is through a mail order company who will have a rapid turn-over of stock. I buy mine in this way and never cease to be delighted with the freshness and fragrance of the goods.

The Essential Indian Spices

Listing all the spices used in Indian cooking would take up many pages of this book so I have picked a selection of the most commonly used, which are essential store-cupboard stock.

Cardamoms – there are two varieties, green and brown. The green ones are more commonly used than the brown and are much smaller. The pods may be used whole, in which case they are often slightly opened at one end to allow the flavor of the seeds to escape. The seeds of the green cardamom may be used without the husks and should be lightly crushed before being added to either sweet or savory dishes. Cardamoms are often used to flavor puddings – Cardamom & Honey Ice Cream (not a classic Indian recipe) is one of my favorite desserts.

Cassia and Cinnamon – these are actually two different spices but they are almost interchangeable, although cassia has a slightly less refined flavor and is therefore more suitable for savory dishes than sweet. Cassia is sometimes called Chinese cinnamon – both are used in Indian cookery.

Chili Powder – adds most of the heat to a dry spice mix. It should be used judiciously until you are an experienced curry cook!

Cilantro/Coriander – this is easy to grow in the garden and grows well on the poorest of ground. It is used in three forms: the cilantro leaves are a fragrant garnish, and the coriander seeds may be used whole (crushed and pressed into lamb leg before roasting they are quite delicious) or ground. The ground spice is mild and is frequently used by the tablespoonful rather than the teaspoon.

Cumin – ground cumin is the basis of many masalas and is immediately identifiable by its fragrance. It is slightly sharp. Cumin seeds are usually roasted to release their flavor before being used.

Mustard Seeds – there are three types: black, brown and white, but it is the white that is most commonly used in Indian cookery. Mustard seeds are used whole or lightly crushed to release their flavor. They make a particularly successful marinade for shellfish such as shrimp.

Poppy Seeds – are not really a spice but they are a valuable flavoring. They may be blue or white and add a distinctive nutty flavor and texture to many dishes. Some recipes call for them to be crushed but I prefer to leave them whole – they are delightful in kormas and other creamy curries.

Turmeric – this is a ground, dried tuber, used for its mild flavor and for its striking yellow color. Often nick-named "poor man's saffron," it should not be used as a coloring in dishes where its distinctive flavor will dominate other ingredients.

Creamed Coconut is not a spice but it is another invaluable store-cupboard ingredient for the avid curry cook. It is sold in a block and is a rich, creamy coconut preparation which should be crumbled before being added to a hot masala or sauce, and then stirred until dissolved. It has a much better flavor and texture than flaked coconut and is easier to use than canned coconut milk. You may have difficulty in getting it, however, and flaked coconut is used in the recipes. Substitute creamed coconut if posssible.

Frying over Low Heat

There are two golden rules for cooking with ground spices. The first is that they must always be cooked in a little hot fat, usually with onions or other vegetables that require pre-cooking, to remove any floury, uncooked flavor. The second rule is that this cooking should take place over very low heat, to ensure that the spices do not burn. Many of the recipes given in this book go to great lengths to explain the heat that should be used for various processes. It is essential that the instructions given are carefully followed to ensure that the best results and flavors are obtained from all the ingredients in any dish. Burnt spices contribute nothing except a bitter aftertaste to a dish.

Salt and Pepper

These essential seasonings are of paramount importance in any cuisine. Salt is especially important in Indian cooking as it brings out the flavors of otherwise bland dishes. I remember in my very early days of demonstrating that I had invited a class to taste a red lentil daal and that there had been very little comment about it. Convinced that it would be as delicious as usual I took a large spoonful as soon as everyone had left and realised immediately that it hadn't even seen the salt pot – it was very dull. Many recipes actually specify the amount of salt to be added to a dish, although it may of course be adjusted to suit your individual taste at the end of the cooking period. As spoon measures in recipes are always taken as level measures you will find that some recipes call for one and a quarter teaspoons of salt – this may easily be converted to one heaped teaspoon.

Before chilies arrived in India in the late fifteenth century – they were native to Mexico and were quickly introduced to other parts of the world by Spanish and Portuguese explorers – most Indian recipes relied on peppercorns for their heat. Indian, or Tellicherry, peppercorns are small and very hot. They are my favorite peppercorns but they need to be finely ground or unsuspecting guests may be surprised by their fire.

Tea – One of India's Greatest Exports

Well, that's my opinion but then I'm a tea addict! India and China are the two greatest quality tea producing nations but India produces more "normal" teas – many China teas are lightly smoked or fermented for extra flavor.

Assam, the region that appears to have been tacked onto the north east of India, produces fine strong teas that are popular throughout the world. Assam is an ideal tea for early morning with its robust flavor and rich brown color. Darjeeling, the champagne tea, is the other great Indian variety. It is grown in the foothills of the Himalayas and has a light, delicate scent and flavor. It is the perfect afternoon tea and is often drunk black. Earl Grey, another of the most popular teas, is actually a blend of Indian and China black teas which is flavored with oil of bergamot. A true Earl Grey blend has to be made with both Indian and China teas – for many years inferior blends were sold containing bergamot and one or other of the black teas but not both.

The classic cuisine of India has so much to offer. There is much more to it than two or three varieties of curry and it may take many years to learn all the secrets of gourmet Indian cookery. Do remember that mild and creamy dishes have just as much to offer as burningly hot ones, and that they will suit the majority of your friends and family much better than the "total experience" dishes! I hope that the selection of classic recipes in this book will be as much of an inspiration to you as it has been to me.

APPETIZERS & SNACKS

For the vast majority of Indians the concept of a meal made up of various courses is virtually unknown. It is an idea that has been adopted by the owners of numerous Indian restaurants to appease western perceptions of how a meal should be served.

Snacks are, however, very popular and whilst many are bought ready-made in the countless street markets in every town, there are some that are best cooked at home. Onion bhajis certainly fall into this category as they need to be piping hot, and served immediately after cooking, to be at their best.

Soup – a Thin Curry

There are surprisingly few soups within the classic Indian cuisine. Perhaps this is because the idea of an appetizer only exists in the homes of the better-off city dwellers, but I feel that the more likely explanation is that a simple dish of dhal is more filling and nutritious than a soup would be. However, those who do eat soup often refer to it as a thin curry, and to a masala as a thick curry.

Samosas, the Perfect Snack

Meat and vegetable samosas have become popular foods available at the delicatessen counters of many modern western supermarkets. They are deep-fried parcels enclosing a spicy filling which are really superb when eaten hot. Samosas are usually triangular in shape and I find the folding and shaping of the pastry to be an art in itself! Unfortunately, the fact that so many supermarkets now sell samosas means that many people eat them cold, when they are quite definitely not at their best, and they never experience the true glory of these delicious snacks.

The first time that I tried a home-made samosa was at a party at the television studios where I was working at the time. They were made by a researcher and were an absolute revelation. I resolved then and there never to buy ready-made samosas again and I never have. I must, however, admit to a certain amount of cheating. There is a recipe for samosa pastry in this book, but you may prefer to use some of the excellent filo pastry that is now available in most supermarkets. Brush the sheets with melted ghee or butter and proceed with the folding and shaping as directed in the recipe. Always allow the stuffing mixture to cool completely before filling the samosas, otherwise the inside of the pastry may sweat and become soggy.

Chicken Tikka – a Popular Restaurant Appetizer

Chicken Tikka is traditionally cooked in a clay oven, a tandoor, and is one of the classic dishes from the Punjab region of northern India. Cubes of marinated spiced chicken are threaded onto skewers and baked quickly, producing a succulent dry spiced dish. I would serve Chicken Tikka with a raita, a tomato or onion salad and puris or other small Indian breads. This recipe provides the base for the extremely popular Chicken Tikka Masala, but do remember to prepare the tikka before embarking on the masala sauce.

Pakoras – Deep-fried Fritters

Another dish originally from the Punjab but which is now popular throughout India is the pakora, a deep-fried fritter, traditionally made with vegetables but left-over cooked chicken is now sometimes used. There is a crisp-like snack available in the west called a pakora but it bears little resemblance to those that I have tasted in good restaurants.

The basic pakora batter is spiced and often contains some whole spices as well as ground. Almost any vegetable can be prepared as a pakora – cauliflower and potato are my favorites – but the secret of success is to ensure that the pieces of vegetable are completely covered with the batter before they are fried. This prevents the vegetables from becoming greasy and ensures even, crisp cooking.

Onion Bhajis – a Favorite Dish

The first time that I made onion bhajis they were an unqualified disaster, simply because I like them so much that I thought I would make big ones – a big mistake! The bhajis are sliced or shredded onions coated in a thick batter and then fried, quite a simple cooking process but one that I totally messed up by making my bhajis too big. As I now know only too well, if they are too large the bhajis will not cook in the middle before they are cooked on the outside, so the golden rule is to keep them only a little larger than bite-size. I can assure you that, in this case, small is best!

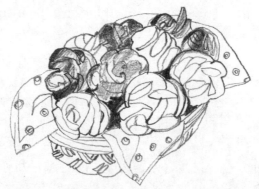

DHAL SOUP

This is a thick warming lentil soup, lightly spiced and suitable for hot and cold days alike.

Serves 6

INGREDIENTS
1½ cups red or yellow lentils
4 cups water or stock
4 canned tomatoes, drained and crushed
1 green chili, sliced lengthwise and de-seeded
2 tbsps plain yogurt or sour cream
1 tbsp butter
1 onion, chopped, or sliced into rings
Salt and freshly ground black pepper
Freshly chopped cilantro leaves to garnish

Wash the lentils in 4-5 changes of water. Drain them well and put them into a large pan with the water or stock. Cover the pan and bring the lentils to a boil over moderate heat. Lower the heat and simmer for about 10-15 minutes, or until the lentils are soft. You may need to add extra water. Using a whisk, beat the lentils until they are smooth. Add the tomatoes and chili and simmer for 2 minutes, then stir in the yogurt or sour cream. Reheat, but do not boil.

Melt the butter in a small pan and fry the onion gently, until it is soft, but not colored.

Pour the soup into serving bowls and scatter with the chopped cilantro and fried onion. Discard the green chilies before eating the soup.

ONION BHAJIS

These Onion Bhajis are one of the most popular appetizers in western Indian restaurants, as well as being firm favorites all over India. They are shredded onions coated in a lightly spiced batter which is then deep-fried.

Serves 6-8

INGREDIENTS
1 cup besan (gram or garbanzo bean flour)
1 tsp salt
Pinch of baking soda
1 tbsp ground rice
2 tsps ground cumin
2 tsps ground coriander
½-1 tsp chili powder
1-2 fresh green chilies, finely chopped and de-seeded if a mild flavor is preferred
2 large onions, sliced into half rings and separated
1 cup water
Oil for deep-frying

Sift the besan and add the salt, baking soda, ground rice, cumin, coriander, chili powder and green chilies; mix well. Add the onions and mix thoroughly, then gradually add the water and keep mixing until a soft but thick batter is formed and the onions are thoroughly coated with the batter.

Heat the oil over medium heat (*it is important to heat the oil to the correct temperature: 325-350°F*). To test the temperature, take a tiny amount of the batter, and drop it in the oil. If it floats up to the surface immediately, but without turning brown, the oil is at the correct temperature. Using a tbsp, add as many half spoonfuls of the onion mix as the pan will hold in a single layer. Take care not to make them too large as this will result in the outside of the bhajis being overdone while the insides remain uncooked, a common problem. Lower the heat as the bhajis need to be fried over a gentle heat to ensure that the batter at the center of the bhajis is cooked, and stays soft, while the outside turns golden brown and crispy. This should take about 10-12 minutes for each batch. Drain the bhajis on paper towels, before serving.

CHICKEN OR TURKEY PAKORAS

I have suggested fresh meat for the recipe below, but you could easily make these pakoras with left-over poultry from a roast.

Serves 6-8

INGREDIENTS
⅔ cup water
1 onion, roughly chopped
2-3 cloves garlic, peeled and roughly chopped
1-2 fresh green chilies, roughly chopped; de-seeded if you prefer a mild flavor
2 tbsps freshly chopped cilantro leaves
1 cup besan (gram flour or garbanzo bean flour), sifted
1 tsp ground coriander
1 tsp ground cumin
½ tsp garam masala
½ tsp chili powder
1 tsp salt
Pinch of baking soda
¾ pound boneless and skinless chicken or turkey breast
Oil for deep-frying

Put 6 tbsps water from the measured amount into a blender with the onion, garlic, green chilies and cilantro leaves, and blend until smooth.

Alternatively, mix the ingredients in a food processor without the water. Mix the besan, coriander, cumin, garam masala, chili powder, salt and baking soda together in a large bowl. Add the blended ingredients and mix thoroughly, then add enough of the remaining water, mixing well, to form a thick paste. Cut the chicken into pieces and add them to the paste, turning until the chicken is well coated.

Heat the oil in in a skillet over medium heat; when hot, add one piece of besan-coated chicken at a time from a tablespoon until there is a single layer without overcrowding. Make certain that each piece is fully coated with the paste before adding it to the skillet. Reduce the heat and fry the pakoras for 10-15 minutes, turning them over halfway through cooking. Remove the pakoras with a slotted spoon and drain on paper towels.

BOTI KEBAB

*Lamb is my favorite meat for curries and other Indian foods.
Serve these kebabs on their skewers as an appetizer or serve
individual pieces of the lamb on cocktail sticks for drinks
party nibbles.*

Serves 6

INGREDIENTS
1½ pounds boneless lamb leg
2 small cloves of garlic, peeled
  and chopped
2 tbsps freshly chopped cilantro
  leaves
2 tbsps lemon juice
6 tbsps thick plain yogurt
Salt
½ tsp ground turmeric
2 tbsps cooking oil

6 green cardamoms (with skin)
1 cinnamon stick, 1 inch long
2-3 dried red chilies
1 tbsp coriander seeds

To Garnish
Thinly sliced onion rings,
  separated
Crisp lettuce leaves
Wedges of cucumber

Prick the meat all over with a
sharp knife and cut into 1½-inch
cubes. Place the garlic, cilantro
leaves, lemon juice and yogurt in
a blender or food processor and
mix until smooth. Add the salt
and turmeric. Grind the

remaining spices together and
add to the yogurt. Put the meat
into a bowl and add the blended
ingredients. Mix thoroughly,
cover, and leave to marinate for
6-8 hours (or overnight in the
refrigerator).

Line the broiler pan with a piece
of foil (this will reflect heat and
also keep your pan clean).
Thread the meat onto skewers,
leaving about a ¼-inch gap
between pieces. Mix any
remaining marinade with the oil.
Place the skewers on the
prepared broiler pan and broil
the kebabs for 2-3 minutes, then
turn and broil for a further 2-3
minutes. Lower the heat. Brush
the kebabs with the oil and
marinade mixture and broil for a
further 6-8 minutes. Turn the
skewers over and baste again
with the remaining marinade
mixture. Broil for a further 6-8
mintues, then serve immediately.

POTATO PAKORAS

Potatoes are my favorite vegetable to make into pakoras – I like the smooth texture hidden inside the crispy, spiced batter.

Serves 4-6

INGREDIENTS

⅓ cup besan (gram flour or garbanzo bean flour)
1 tbsp ground rice
½ tsp salt
1½ tsps ground coriander
1 tsp ground cumin
½ tsp chili powder
¼ cup water
1 pound potatoes, peeled and cut into ¼-inch thick slices
Oil for deep-frying

Mix all the dry ingredients together in a large bowl, then add the water and mix to thick paste. Add the potatoes and mix until the slices are completely coated with the paste.

Heat the oil over medium heat in a deep skillet to about 340°F. Add as many of the coated potato slices as the pan will hold in a single layer. Fry the pakoras until golden brown – about 6-8 minutes. Drain on paper towels before serving.

MEAT SAMOSAS

I find that meat samosas make an excellent light lunch or lunch dish. The first time that I tasted home-made samosas I resolved never to buy ready-made ones again – they are delicious!

Makes 18 samosas

INGREDIENTS
2 tbsps cooking oil
2 onions, finely chopped
½ pound lean ground lamb or beef
3-4 cloves garlic, peeled and crushed
½-inch piece of fresh root ginger, finely grated
½ tsp ground turmeric
2 tsps ground coriander
1½ tsps ground cumin
½-1 tsp chili powder
½ tsp salt
½ cup warm water
1½ cups frozen peas
2 tbsps flaked coconut
1 tsp garam masala
1-2 fresh green chilies, finely chopped and de-seeded if a mild flavor is preferred
2 tbsps freshly chopped cilantro leaves
1 tbsp lemon juice

Heat the oil over medium heat and fry the onions until they are lightly browned. Add the ground meat, garlic and ginger. Stir-fry until all the liquid evaporates, then lower the heat. Add the turmeric, coriander, cumin, chili powder and salt. Stir and cook until the meat is lightly browned. Add the water and the peas, bring to a boil, cover and simmer for 25-30 minutes. If any liquid remains, cook uncovered for 4-5 minutes until the meat is completely dry, stirring frequently. Stir in the coconut, garam masala, green chilies and cilantro leaves. Remove from the heat and add the lemon juice. Cool thoroughly before filling the samosas.

For the Pastry
2 cups all-purpose flour
¼ cup ghee or butter
½ tsp salt
⅓ cup warm water
Oil for deep-frying

Add the butter and salt to the flour and rub in well. Mix to a soft dough by adding the water. Knead until the dough feels soft to the touch. Divide the dough into 9 pieces. Roll into balls between the palms of your hands and then press down to make flat cakes. Roll out into 4-inch circles and cut each into two. Use each semicircle of pastry as one envelope.

Moisten the straight edge with a little warm water, then fold the semicircle of pastry in half to form a triangular cone. Join the straight edges by pressing them hard into each other. Make sure that there are no gaps. Add the filling, leaving a small border at the top of the cone, then moisten the top edges and press them hard together. Deep-fry the samosas over gentle heat until they are golden brown. Drain on paper towels.

SEEKH KEBABS

Seekh kebabs were the first Indian kebabs that I ever tried and I have been a fan ever since! They can be cooked on metal skewers, but the bamboo type are much more convenient.

Makes 18 kebabs

INGREDIENTS

Juice of ½ lemon
2 tbsps freshly chopped fresh mint *or* 1 tsp dried mint
3-4 tbsps freshly chopped cilantro leaves
⅓ cup raw cashews
1 onion, roughly chopped
2 small cloves of garlic, peeled and roughly chopped
1-2 fresh green chilies, finely chopped or minced; de-seeded if you prefer a mild flavor
1½ pounds lean ground meat, beef or lamb
2 tsps ground coriander
2 tsps ground cumin
1 tsp ground ajwain (ajowan or carum) or ground caraway seeds
½ tsp garam masala
½ tsp tandoori color *or* a few drops of red food coloring mixed with 1 tbsp tomato paste
½ tsp freshly ground black pepper
1 egg yolk
¼ tsp chili powder
1 tsp salt
2 tbsps ground white poppy seeds, ground
2 tbsps ground sesame seeds
4 tbsps cooking oil

Place the lemon juice, mint, cilantro leaves, cashews, onion, garlic and green chilies in a blender or food processor and mix to a smooth paste. Transfer the mixture to a large bowl. Using the blender or processor, mix the ground meat in 2-3 small batches until it is fairly smooth, rather like a paste. Add the meat to the rest of the blended ingredients in the bowl. Add the remaining ingredients, except the oil, and knead the mixture thoroughly until it is smooth. Alternatively, put all the ingredients, except the oil, in an electric food processor and mix until the mixture is smooth. Chill for 30 minutes.

Line a roasting pan with foil. Divide the kebab mix into 18 pieces, form each piece into a sausage shape around a wooden skewer by rolling it between your hands. Place in the prepared roasting pan. Make the rest of the kebabs in the same way. Brush generously with the oil and place the pan in a 475°F oven just below the top. Cook for 6-8 minutes. Remove the pan from the oven and brush the kebabs liberally with the remaining oil. Cook for a further 6-8 minutes.

Allow the kebabs to cool slightly before removing them from the skewers, or serve them on the skewers.

NARGISI KEBABS

These tasty meat balls with a surprise filling are more like patties than kebabs. Use finely ground beef or lamb as coarser meat will split during cooking and allow the filling to escape.

Makes 14 kebabs

INGREDIENTS
For the Filling
2 hard-boiled eggs, shelled and roughly chopped
1 fresh green chili, finely chopped; de-seeded if you prefer a mild flavor
2 tbsps finely chopped onion
1 tbsp finely chopped cilantro leaves
¼ tsp salt
1 tbsp thick plain yogurt

2 tbsps ghee or sweet butter
1 large onion, coarsely chopped
3-4 cloves garlic, peeled and roughly chopped
1-inch piece of fresh root ginger, peeled and roughly chopped

1 tsp ground cumin
1½ tsps ground coriander
1 tsp garam masala
½ tsp chili powder
½ tsp freshly ground black pepper
3 tbsps thick plain yogurt
1 tbsp fresh mint leaves *or* 1 tsp dried mint
2 tbsps freshly chopped cilantro leaves
¾ tsp salt
1¼ pounds lean lamb or beef, finely ground
1 egg
2 tbsps besan (garbanzo bean flour or gram flour), sifted
1 tbsp water
6 tbsps cooking oil

Combine all ingredients for the filling in a bowl, mix thoroughly and put to one side. Melt the ghee or butter over medium heat and fry the onion, garlic and ginger for 3-4 minutes. Lower the heat and add the cumin, coriander, garam masala, chili powder and pepper. Stir-fry for 1-2 minutes, then remove from the heat and let cool.

Place the yogurt in a blender or food processor and add the fried ingredients, the mint, cilantro, salt and the meat. Blend until smooth. If you are using a blender, mix the ingredients first without the meat. Transfer the blended ingredients to a mixing bowl and process the meat in 2-3 batches. Knead the blended ingredients and the meat until smooth. Divide the mixture into portions. Make a depression in the center of each ball and form into a cup shape. Fill with 1 heaped tsp of the egg mixture and cover the filling by pressing the edges together. Roll gently between the palms of your hands to form a neat ball, press the ball gently and form a round flat cake about ¾-inch thick. Make the rest of the kebabs in the same way.

Beat the egg and gradually add the besan while still beating. Add the water and beat again. Heat the oil in a wide, shallow skillet, preferably non-stick or cast iron, over medium heat. Dip each kebab in the egg batter and fry in a single layer without overcrowding the pan. Cook for 3-4 minutes on each side until browned. Drain on paper towels before serving.

CAULIFLOWER PAKORAS

A pakora is a spicy Indian snack, fried in a light batter until crispy. Serve plain as finger food, or with a salad garnish and relishes as an appetizer.

Serves 4

INGREDIENTS
½ cup besan (gram flour or garbanzo bean flour), sifted
1 tbsp ground rice
¾ tsp salt
2 tbsps ground coriander
2 tsps ground cumin
½-1 tsp chili powder
½ tsp ground turmeric
Pinch of baking soda
1 cauliflower, cut into 1½-inch flowerets
⅔ cup water
Oil for deep-frying

Mix all the dry ingredients in a large bowl, then add the cauliflower and water. Mix until the cauliflower is fully coated with the batter.

Heat the oil over medium heat to around 340°F and add as many flowerets as the pan will hold in a single layer. Fry until the pakoras are uniformly brown – this will take about 5 minutes. Drain on paper towels, and serve hot.

SPICED MIXED NUTS

Anyone addicted to dry roasted peanuts will adore these spiced nuts! They might keep in a screw-top jar if given the chance!

Serves 8-10

INGREDIENTS
⅔ cup whole almonds
⅔ cup raw cashews
2 tsps cooking oil
½ tsp ground coriander
½ tsp ground cumin
¼ tsp chili powder
½ tsp salt

Cook the nuts for 3-4 minutes in a heavy based skillet over low heat until the nuts are just heated through. Add 1 tsp oil, stir and mix thoroughly. Toast the nuts until they are evenly browned, stirring constantly. This may take up to 10 minutes. Remove from the heat and sprinkle with the spices and salt immediately. Mix thoroughly, then leave for 10 minutes. Add the remaining oil, stir and mix until the nuts are fully coated with the spices.

Allow to cool completely before serving.

SPICED POTATO BITES

Potatoes are not just a vegetable to serve with meat in Indian cookery! They are used in many inventive ways, such as this cocktail nibble of spiced potatoes, to be served on sticks with drinks.

Serves 6-8

INGREDIENTS
1½ pounds potatoes
4 tbsps cooking oil
½ tbsp salt
¼ tsp garam masala
½ tsp ground cumin
½ tsp ground coriander
¼-½ tsp chili powder

Boil the potatoes in their skins; cool, then peel and dice into 1-inch cubes. Heat the oil over medium heat in a wide shallow skillet, preferably non-stick or cast iron. It is important to have the right pan, otherwise the potatoes will stick. Add the potatoes and spread them evenly around the pan. Brown the potatoes evenly, stirring them occasionally. When the potatoes are brown, sprinkle them with the salt, garam masala, cumin, coriander and chili powder. Stir gently until the potatoes are fully coated with the spices. Remove from the heat, and serve on cocktail sticks or with a salad garnish.

VEGETABLE SAMOSAS

These popular parcels of spicy vegetables are now available in many supermarkets and delicatessens. It really is worth making your own – they are so much better!

Makes 18 samosas

INGREDIENTS
1 pound potatoes
2 tbsps cooking oil
½ tsp black mustard seeds
1 tsp cumin seeds
2 dried red chilies, roughly chopped
1 onion, finely chopped
1-2 fresh green chilies, roughly chopped and de-seeded if a mild flavor is preferred
½ tsp ground turmeric
1 tsp ground coriander
1 tsp ground cumin
1 tsp salt
1 tbsp freshly chopped cilantro leaves
Samosa pastry; see Meat Samosas

Boil the potatoes in their skins, let them cool then peel and dice them. Heat the oil and add the mustard seeds. As soon as they start crackling, add the cumin seeds and red chilies, and then the onions and green chilies. Fry until the onions are soft, then add the turmeric, coriander and cumin. Stir quickly and add the potatoes and the salt. Lower the heat, and stir-fry until the potatoes are thoroughly mixed with the spices. Remove from the heat and stir in the cilantro leaves. Cool thoroughly before filling the samosas. Make up the pastry and complete the Samosas following the method for Meat Samosas.

BARRAH KEBAB (MARINATED LAMB STEAKS)

This delicious spiced lamb dish may be served as an appetizer or a main course. The yogurt tenderizes the lamb before cooking.

Serves 6-8

INGREDIENTS

2 pounds lamb leg steaks
½ tsp ground nutmeg
½ tsp ground black pepper
½ tsp ground cinnamon
½ tsp cayenne or chili powder
½ tsp ground turmeric
2 cloves garlic, peeled
2 tbsps roughly chopped onions
½-inch piece of fresh root ginger, peeled and chopped
⅔ cup thick plain yogurt
½ tsp salt
1 tbsp cooking oil
1 tsp ground cumin
1 tbsp sesame seeds

Trim off any excess fat from the steaks and flatten each one with a meat mallet or a rolling pin. Place all ingredients except the steaks, oil, cumin and sesame seeds into a blender or food processor and blend to a purée. Place the steaks in a large bowl and pour the blended ingredients over them. Rub the marinade into each steak with your fingers, then cover and leave to marinate for at least 8 hours in a cool place or overnight in the refrigerator.

Line a roasting pan with foil (this will help reflect heat and keep your roasting pan clean). Arrange the steaks in the pan in a single layer (reserve any remaining marinade) and cook in the centre of a 425°F oven for 10 minutes – turn the steaks over once. Lower the heat to 400°F. Mix the remaining marinade with the oil and cumin. Brush the steaks with this and sprinkle half the sesame seeds on top. Return the pan to the upper part of the oven for 10 minutes. Turn the steaks over and brush with the remaining marinade mixture, adding the rest of the sesame seeds as before. Cook for a further 10-15 minutes, until the meat is tender.

MUTTON PATTIES

These little mutton patties are now most commonly made with lamb, although beef could be used if preferred. Serve with a tomato and onion salad and relishes.

Makes 14 patties

INGREDIENTS
2¼ pounds potatoes
½-1 tsp chili powder
1½ tsps salt
3 tbsps cooking oil
½ tsp fennel seeds
1 large onion, finely chopped
½-inch piece of fresh root ginger, peeled and finely grated
2-4 cloves garlic, peeled and chopped or crushed
¾ pound fine lean ground lamb

1 tsp ground cumin
1½ tsps ground coriander
1 tsp ground fennel
½ tsp ground turmeric
½ tsp garam masala
3 tbsps water

7-ounce can tomatoes
⅓ cup water
1 fresh green chili, finely chopped
2 tbsps freshly chopped cilantro leaves
1 egg, beaten
2 tbsps milk
2 tbsps flour
1½.cups golden breadcrumbs
Oil for deep-frying

Boil the potatoes in their skins, cool slightly, then peel and mash them. Add half the chili powder and ½ tsp salt from the measured amount. Divide the mixture into 14 portions, cover and put on one side. Heat the oil over medium heat and fry the fennel seeds until brown. Add the onions, ginger and garlic, and fry until the onions are lightly browned. Add the meat and fry for 5 minutes or so until all moisture evaporates, stirring frequently. Mix the spices with the water and add to the pan. Cook for 5-6 minutes, lowering the heat for the last 2-3 minutes. Raise the heat and add the tomatoes, breaking them up with the back of a spoon. Cook for 3-4 minutes, stirring frequently. Add the water, the remaining chili powder and salt, then cover and simmer for 15 minutes. Cook, uncovered, for a further 4-5 minutes or until the mixture is completely dry but moist. Stir frequently. Stir in the chopped green chili and the cilantro leaves. Cook for 1-2 minutes, then remove from the heat and let cool completely.

Mix the beaten egg with the milk and put on one side. Take a portion of the potato and roll it into a ball. Make a depression in the center and form into a cup shape. Fill the cavity with some of the mixture, leaving a border around the filling. Ease the potato around the meat to enclose the filling completely, then flatten to form a round cake, about ½ inch thick. Use the potato and meat to make 14 patties. Dust the patties in the flour; then dip in egg and milk mixture and roll in the breadcrumbs. Deep-fry the patties for about 6-8 minutes until they are golden brown. Drain on paper towels.

CHICKEN TIKKA

Of all the Indian restaurant appetizers I think that this is the most popular! It should be cooked in a tandoor, an Indian clay oven, but this recipe is adapted for a standard oven.

Serves 4

INGREDIENTS
1 pound boneless chicken breast, skinned
1 tsp salt
Juice of ½ lemon
½ tsp tandoori color *or* a few drops of red food coloring mixed with 1 tbsp tomato paste
2 cloves garlic, peeled and roughly chopped
½-inch piece of fresh root ginger, peeled and roughly chopped
2 tsps ground coriander
½ tsp ground allspice or garam masala
¼ a whole nutmeg, finely grated
½ tsp ground turmeric
⅔ cup thick plain yogurt
¼ cup corn or vegetable oil
½ tsp chili powder

Cut the chicken into 1-inch cubes. Sprinkle with ½ tsp salt from the measured amount and the lemon juice. Mix thoroughly, cover and leave for 30 minutes. Place the rest of the ingredients in a blender or food processor and mix until smooth. Strain the sauce over the chicken through a strainer – force the mixture through using the back of a spoon and discard anything left.

Coat the chicken thoroughly with the strained marinade, cover, and leave to marinate for 6-8 hours or overnight in the refrigerator.

Line a roasting pan with foil (this will help to maintain the high level of temperature required to cook the chicken quickly without drying it out). Thread the chicken pieces onto skewers, leaving a ¼-inch gap between pieces (this is necessary for the heat to reach all sides of the chicken). Place the skewers in the prepared roasting pan and brush with some of the remaining marinade. Cook in the center of a 450°F oven for 6-8 minutes. Turn the skewers over and brush the pieces of chicken with the remaining marinade. Return the pan to the oven and cook for a further 6-8 minutes. Shake off any excess liquid from the chicken. (Strain the excess liquid and keep aside for Chicken Tikka Masala.) Place the skewers on a serving dish. You may take the tikka off the skewers if you wish, but let the meat cool slightly before removing it from the skewers.

DHINGRI KARI (MUSHROOM CURRY)

This mushroom curry is not too hot but does have a fairly robust flavor. I would serve it with brown rice as an appetizer.

Serves 4

INGREDIENTS
½ cup finely sliced leeks
2 cloves garlic, peeled and crushed
½ tsp fresh root ginger, peeled and grated
2 tsps curry powder
1 tsp garam masala
2 tbsps oil
1 pound mushrooms, cut into quarters
1 cup flaked coconut
1 tbsp lemon juice
Salt

Fry the leeks, garlic, ginger and spices in the oil until soft. Add the mushrooms and cook over low heat until soft. Grind the flaked coconut in a coffee grinder or a pestle and mortar to a fine texture. Add the coconut and cook gently until it is completely dissolved, adding a little water if the mixture appears too dry. Stir in the lemon juice and sufficient salt to taste. Serve on a bed of rice.

FISH & SHELLFISH

I am certain that most people who have eaten in an Indian restaurant have tried a shrimp masala or a shrimp biryani. I have no figures to support my theory but I am certain that shrimp is second only to chicken as the most popular main ingredient in restaurant curries.

The Ubiquitous Shrimp
Excellent shrimp are caught off the Indian coast and they are often exported as their quality is so good. They range in size from tiny right up to enormous jumbo shrimp, sometimes weighing up to a pound each. Such a range of sizes has

allowed a vast number of shrimp recipes to be developed over the years. The smaller shrimp, the ones of a size most familiar to us, make the best curries as they can easily be coated with a sauce, completely absorbing the flavors and becoming a deliciously integrated dish. Larger shrimp may be scattered with spices and brushed with oil, then baked or grilled. Shrimp are sometimes marinated in yogurt and spices (mustard seed works particularly well) but my favorite way of cooking them is with onion, garlic, green chilies and coconut. I add some pickles and tomato paste and, within 10 minutes, I have a dish that is utterly delicious.

Tasty as they are it is, however, a great pity that shrimp are so totally dominant as a fish in the average Indian restaurant. I can understand why – they are still considered to be a treat (hence the enduring popularity of the shrimp cocktail) but there are many other fish which I feel make better curries than these endlessly popular shellfish.

The best Indian fish dish that I have ever tasted was a baked mackerel, served as part of a Sunday lunch-time buffet in an Indian restaurant near my home. Mackerel are caught off the south east coast of India and their robust flavor and firm texture are the perfect medium for spicy, Indian cooking. The mackerel was cooked in a similar way to the recipe for Spiced Sardines and was absolutely delicious – any oily fish would cook well in this way; herrings in season would make a delicious and very economical dish.

Pomfret – an Indian Speciality

Pomfret is highly prized in all eastern cookery and is the ultimate fish for Indian cooking. It is the most extraordinary and distinctive fish to look at, having an almost translucent whiteness to its flesh – in a fresh fish shop, among other fish with the more common brown, grey or pinky-orange skins, it shimmers and demands to be noticed. It is a flat fish with a sharply forked tail and distinctive fins, the skin graduating from a shimmering grey to an almost pure white on the belly.

Pomfret has a texture that is similar to turbot and it is often cooked with fresh cilantro leaves, chilies and a paste of ginger and garlic. The classic way to cook the fish is by wrapping it in banana leaves before baking or steaming it – foil just doesn't give the same result.

Under Rather than Over

The most important rule when cooking fish is to cook it quickly, so as not to lose all the moisture from the flesh, resulting in a dry, unpalatable dish. It almost takes longer to assemble and prepare the ingredients for the majority of recipes in this chapter than it does to cook them! Always under-cook fish rather than over-cook it – it will probably be done to perfection by the time you have served the dish and presented it to your family and friends.

When is a Duck a Fish?

When it's a Bombay Duck! You will know if you have ever been in close proximity to one of these – the smell is unmistakable! Bombay Duck is dried bombil, a small fish caught in huge quantities in Indian waters, especially off Bombay hence the name. The fish are dried in the sun and provide a cheap form of protein for many Indian people. In the west, they are served as an accompaniment to curries and other Indian dishes. In India, Bombay Duck often provides all the protein in a meal and, dried or fresh, it is made into many different dishes. You may occasionally get Bombay Duck in a fresh fish shop, but it is more usually found in a specialist Indian shop or delicatessen. I find it too strong a flavor, but friends of mine who are addicts run it under cold water and then bake it briefly in the oven to soften the flesh before eating it. It's all a matter of taste!

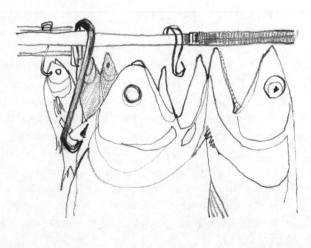

SHRIMP CHILI MASALA

Jumbo shrimp are favored for curries in India, but any large frozen shrimp may be used in this dish.

Serves 4

INGREDIENTS

6 tbsps sweet butter
6 green cardamoms, the top of each pod split open
1-inch piece of fresh root ginger, peeled and finely grated
3-4 cloves garlic, peeled and crushed
1 tbsp ground coriander
½ tsp ground turmeric
1 pound peeled shrimp
⅔ cup thick plain yogurt
⅓ cup water
1 tsp sugar
1 tsp salt
¼ cup ground almonds
4-6 whole fresh green chilies
½ cup finely chopped onions
2 fresh green chilies, de-seeded and finely chopped
½ tsp garam masala
1 tbsp freshly chopped cilantro leaves

Melt 4 tbsps of butter over gentle heat and add the whole cardamoms; fry for 30 seconds, then add the ginger and garlic. Stir and cook for 1 minute, then add the ground coriander and turmeric. Stir-fry for 30 seconds. Add the shrimp, turn up the heat and cook for 3-4 minutes, stirring frequently.

Beat the yogurt until smooth, gradually adding the water. Add this mixture to the shrimp with the sugar and the salt, cover the pan and simmer for 5-6 minutes. Add the ground almonds and the whole green chilies and cook, uncovered, for 5 minutes.

Meanwhile, fry the onions in the remaining butter until they are just soft, but not brown. Add the chopped green chilies and the garam masala and cook for a further 1-2 minutes. Stir this mixture into the shrimp with any butter left in the pan. Turn the shrimp into a warmed serving dish and garnish with the cilantro leaves.

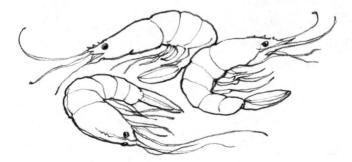

FISH BHOONA

A bhoona is a fairly spicy curry, sometimes hot and sometimes medium, cooked in hot oil, which removes any floury dryness from the spices.

Serves 4

INGREDIENTS

1½ pounds white fish fillets or steaks
6 tbsps cooking oil

1 tbsp all-purpose flour
¼ tsp ground turmeric
¼ tsp chili powder
¼ tsp salt

1 large onion, roughly chopped
½-inch piece of fresh root ginger, peeled and roughly chopped
2-4 cloves garlic, peeled and roughly chopped
½ tsp ground turmeric
¼ tsp chili powder
1 tsp ground coriander
½ tsp garam masala
7-ounce can tomatoes
⅔ cup warm water
1 cup frozen peas
1 tsp salt
1 tbsp freshly chopped cilantro leaves

Skin the fish, rinse and dry thoroughly on paper towels, then cut the fish into approximately 1 × 2-inch pieces. Heat 2 tbsps of the oil in a large skillet, preferably non-stick or cast iron, over medium heat. Mix the flour with the seasonings, then lightly dust the fish, one piece at a time, in the seasoned flour and place in the hot oil. Put in as many pieces as the pan will hold in a single layer. Turn up the heat slightly and fry the fish until all the pieces are evenly browned. This has to be done quickly in fairly hot oil so that the fish is thoroughly sealed. Fry all the fish in this way and drain on paper towels.

Place the onion, ginger and garlic in a blender or food processor and mix until smooth. Heat the remaining oil in a wide, shallow pan, over medium heat. Add the onion mixture and cook for 3-4 minutes, lowering the heat as necessary. Add the turmeric, chili, coriander and garam masala and fry for 4-5 minutes, stirring continuously. Add the juice from the tomatoes, a little at a time, to prevent the spices from sticking to the base of the pan. Add the tomatoes and cook for 2-3 minutes, breaking them up with a spoon and mixing them into the other ingredients. Add the water, peas and salt. Bring to a boil and add the fish. Cover and simmer for 5-6 minutes. Garnish the bhoona with the cilantro leaves and serve.

COD CURRY

This is really two recipes in one! It's up to you to decide whether to use yogurt or tomatoes as both are delicious.

Serves 4

INGREDIENTS
1 large onion, chopped
3 tbsps vegetable oil
1-inch piece cinnamon stick
1 bay leaf
½-inch piece root ginger, peeled and grated
2-3 cloves garlic, peeled and crushed
1 tsp chili powder
1 tsp ground cumin
1 tsp ground coriander
¼ tsp ground turmeric
⅔ cup plain yogurt *or* 7-ounce can tomatoes, chopped
1-2 fresh green chilies, chopped
1 tbsp freshly chopped cilantro leaves
1 pound cod cutlets, or fillets, cut into 2-inch pieces
1 tsp salt

Fry the onion in the oil in a large heavy based pan until golden brown. Add the cinnamon, bay leaf, ginger and garlic and fry for 1 minute. Add the ground spices and fry for a further minute over low heat, then stir in either the yogurt or the canned tomatoes and then the chopped chilies and cilantro. Only if you have used yogurt, stir in ⅔ cup water and simmer the mixture for 2-3 minutes. Do not add any water if you have used canned tomatoes. Stir the cod into the sauce, and add the salt. Cover the pan and simmer for 10-15 minutes before serving.

TANDOORI FISH

Firm white fish fillets are ideal for Tandoori Fish, although I have cooked the recipe most successfully using mackerel fillets.

Serves 4

INGREDIENTS

1 pound white fish fillets or steaks

½ tsp salt

Small piece of fresh root ginger, peeled and coarsely chopped

2 cloves garlic, peeled and roughly chopped

1 tsp ground cumin

1 tsp ground coriander

½ tsp garam masala

¼-½ tsp chili powder

¼ tsp tandoori color *or* a few drops of red food coloring mixed with 1 tbsp tomato paste

Juice of ½ lemon

3 tbsps water

2 tbsps cooking oil

2 heaped tbsps all-purpose flour

½ tsp chili powder

¼ tsp salt

Rinse the fish and dry on paper towels. Cut into 1-inch squares. Add the salt to the ginger and garlic and crush to a smooth pulp; then mix with the cumin, coriander, garam masala, chili powder and tandoori color or tomato paste mix. Add the lemon juice and water and mix thoroughly. Put to one side.

Heat the oil in a non-stick or cast iron skillet over medium heat. Mix the flour, chili powder and salt. Dust each piece of fish in the seasoned flour and put in the hot oil in a single layer – leave plenty of room in the pan. Fry for 5 minutes, turning once, then drain on paper towels. Return all the fish to the pan. Hold a sifter over the pan and pour the liquid spice mixture into it. Press with the back of a metal spoon until only dry waste is left in the sifter – discard this. Stir the spices gently into the fish and cook over medium heat until the fish is fully coated with the spices and the liquid dries up. Serve immediately.

MASALA MACHCHI

Masala Machchi is a medium hot, spicy fish dish, strongly flavored with lemon juice.

Serves 4

INGREDIENTS
Juice of ½ lemon
1 small onion, roughly chopped
2-3 cloves garlic, peeled and
 roughly chopped
1-inch piece of fresh root ginger,
 peeled and roughly chopped
1-2 fresh green chilies, chopped;
 de-seeded if you like a mild
 flavor
3 tbsps freshly chopped cilantro
 leaves
1 tsp salt
1 pound white fish fillets
6 tbsps oil for shallow-frying
Lemon slices for garnish

Coating
3 tbsps all-purpose flour
¼ tsp salt
¼ tsp chili powder
1 egg, beaten

Place the lemon juice, onion, garlic, ginger, green chilies, cilantro leaves and 1 tsp of salt in a blender or food processor and mix until smooth. Rinse the fish and pat dry with paper towels. Cut the fish into 1½ × 1-inch pieces. Brush a light coating of the spice paste onto all sides of each piece of fish. Cover and leave to marinate in a cool place for 2-3 hours, or overnight in the refrigerator.

Mix the flour for frying with the salt and chili powder. Dust each piece of fish lightly with the mixture, then dip in the beaten egg. Shallow-fry in a single layer over medium heat until the fish is brown on both sides – 2-3 minutes on each side. Drain on paper towels. Alternatively, deep-fry the fish until golden brown and drain on paper towels. Serve garnished with slices of lemon.

SPICED SARDINES

This recipe combines some of my favorite flavors in a lightly spiced curry, especially if served with an avocado relish.

Serves 4

INGREDIENTS

8 fresh sardines (about 1½ pounds)
1 tsp salt
3-4 cloves garlic, peeled and roughly chopped
Juice of ½ lemon
½ tsp ground turmeric
½-1 tsp chili powder
3 tbsps all-purpose flour
4 tbsps cooking oil·

Scale and clean the fish. Rinse in cold water and dry on paper towels.

Add the salt to the garlic and work to a smooth pulp. Mix all the remaining ingredients except the fish, flour and oil together in a small bowl. Place the fish in a wide shallow dish and pour the marinade over. Spread it gently over both sides of the fish, then cover and chill for 2-4 hours.

Heat the oil over medium heat. Dip each fish in the flour and coat it thoroughly. Fry until golden brown on both sides – this will take 2-3 minutes a side. Drain on paper towels.

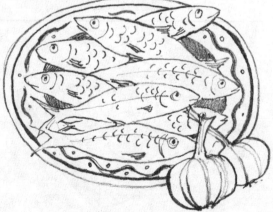

COD ROE SCRAMBLE

This highly nutritious dish is lightly spiced, which takes away much of the richness of the roe.

Serves 4

INGREDIENTS
½ pound fresh cod roe
2 tbsps cooking oil
1 onion, finely chopped
1 fresh green chili, finely
  chopped
2 tbsps ground coriander
½ tsp ground turmeric
½ tsp salt

Chop the cod roe roughly. Heat the oil in a non-stick or cast iron skillet over medium heat and fry the onion and green chili until the onion is soft but not brown. Add the coriander and turmeric. Stir, and cook for 1 minute; then add the cod roe and salt. Cook for 3-4 minutes, breaking up the pieces of roe with a spoon. Lower the heat and cook until the roe begins to brown, stirring occasionally. Remove from the heat and serve.

SARDINE FRY

The fish for this appetizer are fried whole.

Serves 4

INGREDIENTS
½ pound cleaned small sardines
¼ tsp turmeric
1 tsp chili powder
1 tsp salt
Oil for deep-frying
Lemon juice

Rub the sardines well with turmeric, chili powder and salt. Gently heat the oil and fry the fish for 6-8 minutes, a few at a time, until crispy. Drain on paper towels, then sprinkle with lemon juice and serve.

SHRIMP CURRY

This is a hot, slightly sour shrimp curry, delicious with plain boiled rice and a yogurt dressing.

Serves 4

INGREDIENTS
1 large onion, chopped
4 tbsps ghee *or* 3 tbsps oil
1-inch cinnamon stick
6 green cardamoms
6 cloves
1 bay leaf
1 tsp fresh root ginger, peeled and grated
2-3 cloves garlic, peeled and crushed
1 tsp chili powder
1 tsp ground cumin
1 tsp ground coriander
½ tsp salt
1 green pepper, de-seeded and cut into ½-inch pieces
7-ounce can tomatoes, crushed
1 pound large peeled shrimp
1 tbsp freshly chopped cilantro leaves
2 green chilies, chopped

Fry the onions in ghee or oil until soft, then add the cinnamon, cardamoms, cloves and bay leaf. Fry for 1 minute, and then add ginger and garlic, chili, cumin, coriander and salt. Fry for 30 seconds. Add the chopped green pepper and tomatoes, then bring to a boil and add the shrimp. Return the mixture to a boil and cook for 10-15 minutes. Garnish with the chopped cilantro and chopped chilies.

BENGAL FISH CURRY

There is an abundance of fish in the Bay of Bengal and the people of this region of India are masters of the art of fish curries.

Serves 4

INGREDIENTS

1½ pounds firm fleshed fish such as river trout
1 tsp ground turmeric
1¼ tsps salt
5 tbsps cooking oil
1 large onion, finely chopped
Small piece of fresh root ginger, peeled and finely chopped or grated
1 tbsp ground coriander
½-1 tsp chili powder
1 tsp paprika pepper
1¼ cups thick plain yogurt
4-6 whole fresh green chilies
1-2 cloves of garlic, peeled and crushed
1 tbsp besan (gram or garbanzo bean flour)
2 tbsps freshly chopped cilantro leaves

Clean and skin the fish; wash and pat dry. Cut each fish into 1½-inch pieces, and remove as many bones as possible. Gently rub a little of the turmeric and salt over the fish, then leave it for 15-20 minutes.

Meanwhile, heat the oil over medium heat in a skillet wide enough to hold the fish in a single layer. Fry the onion and ginger until the onion is lightly browned, stirring frequently. Add the coriander, the remaining turmeric, chili powder and the paprika, lower the heat and cook for 1-2 minutes, stirring continuously. Beat the yogurt with a fork until smooth and add to the pan with the whole green chilies, the remaining salt and the garlic. Turn up the heat slightly and mix well. Arrange the pieces of fish in the pan in a single layer and bring to a gentle boil. Cover, and cook over low heat for 5-6 minutes.

Blend the besan with a little water to give a pouring consistency. Strain the mixture into the fish curry and stir gently to mix. Cover and cook for 2-3 minutes. Remove the pan from the heat and gently mix in half the cilantro leaves. Transfer the fish curry to a warmed serving dish and garnish with the remaining cilantro leaves.

FISH SHAHJAHANI

This rich fish curry is named after the gourmet Mughal Emperor Shahjahan, widely acknowledged for his love of good food. Serve with plain or mildly flavored rice.

Serves 4

INGREDIENTS
1½ pounds white fish fillets
½ cup roasted cashews
½ cup light single cream
⅓ cup sweet butter
1 cup finely sliced onions
2-inch piece of cinnamon stick, broken up
4 green cardamoms, the top of each pod split open
2 whole cloves
1-2 fresh green chilies, sliced lengthwise; de-seeded if a mild flavor is preferred
1 tsp ground turmeric
¾ cup warm water
1 tsp salt
1 tbsp lemon juice

Rinse the fish in cold water, dry on paper towels and cut into 1 × 2-inch pieces. Place the cashews and cream in a blender or food processor and mix to a paste.

Melt the butter in a wide, shallow pan over medium heat and fry the onions, cinnamon, cardamom, cloves and green chilies until the onions are lightly browned. Stir in the turmeric, then add the water and salt and arrange the fish in a single layer. Bring to a boil, then cover the pan and simmer for 2-3 minutes. Add the cashew paste and stir gently until all the pieces of fish are well coated. Cover the pan again and simmer for a further 2-3 minutes. Gently stir in the lemon juice before serving.

CHICKEN

Chickens are popular the world over. They blend well with so many flavorings, are quick to cook and succulent – well, that would be a fair description of the chickens of the west. Murghi, their Indian cousins, are not of the same quality and are often quite scrawny, although they do have lots of free-range flavor. Chickens are survivors and in many countries they are left to scratch around for their food in the fields and, indeed, in towns. Progress dictates that battery farming will be introduced in most countries before long and some chicken farms now exist in India, producing better birds for eating. These farms are for both chickens and eggs and it is interesting to note that some vegetarians who would previously not eat eggs will now eat eggs from these farms as their eggs are unfertilized.

Classic Dishes from North and South

Chicken plays an important rôle in just about every great classic cuisine. Some of the best known Indian chicken dishes come from opposite ends of the country. Unless Indians are vegetarian there are no religious reasons to prevent them from eating chicken. The only problem may be that it is too expensive for everyday dishes – for many people chicken is an expensive treat.

Some of the best known of all Indian dishes originate in the Punjab region of northern India, the home of the tandoor oven. The Punjabis are the cooks and gourmets of India and their tandoori dishes are known throughout the world. Tandoori chicken is always marinated in a mixture of spices and yogurt and the best results are obtained when the meat is marinated overnight. The secret of successful tandoori cooking is very quick baking in a hot tandoor, a clay oven. It is difficult to reproduce the exact flavor and texture of the tandoor at home, but a reasonable attempt may be made by cooking in a conventional oven at its highest temperature. Chicken baked in a tandoor is succulent and juicy on the inside but has a dry, slightly crusty outer surface. Naan breads, one of the few leavened breads of India made with yeast, are cooked in the same oven – the Punjabis eat far more bread than the people of the south as the north is wheat and not rice country.

Creamy Kormas from the South

One of the best dishes to cook when first introducing friends or family to Indian cookery is a korma, a mild creamy dish with yogurt and cream in the sauce, which is often thickened with ground almonds and seasoned with saffron. A well made korma is truly a gourmet's delight. Such dishes originate in the south of India and are more commonly served with rice than breads, although pieces of chapati are excellent for scooping up all the delicious sauce. I frequently put a tablespoon or so of blue poppy seeds in a korma – I love the nutty texture and extra color that they give to the sauce.

Some people cook lamb or mutton as a korma but I never feel that this is as successful as chicken – the white meat complements the creamy sauce more readily and naturally.

Other Poultry and Game Birds

Chicken is not the only bird to enjoy a place in the classic cooking of India – duck and goose are also eaten but are reserved for special occasions. Of the game birds, partridge is a special favorite, reserved for the grandest of celebrations. Chicken is really the only poultry to be eaten in any quantity and for many of the people of India even that is a luxury.

Chicken is one of the few major ingredients that really works well with almost any seasonings or ingredients. I have been lyrical about the mildest of curries, the korma and the gourmet dishes of the tandoor, but I should say that chicken cooks just as well as a vindaloo, a very hot sour curry cooked with a little vinegar to give a unique (and tongue tingling) flavor. A flick through this chapter will reveal recipes for Masalas, Makkhani (a very rich butter sauce), and Kohlapuri, a hot chili-based recipe from the south of India. The recipe for Chicken Chaat, in which the chicken pieces are very lightly spiced and stir-fried, is one of the simplest of Indian recipes and is every bit as delightful as some of the more complicated dishes. Such is the versatility of chicken.

CORIANDER CHICKEN

This is a good curry to serve at an Indian dinner party. After the chicken has been marinated the curry cooks quickly and requires little attention. Garnish with fresh cilantro leaf for extra flavor.

Serves 6

INGREDIENTS
6 chicken joints, skinned
2-4 cloves garlic, peeled and
  crushed
⅔ cup thick plain yogurt
5 tbsps cooking oil
1 large onion, finely sliced
2 tbsps ground coriander
½ tsp ground black pepper
1 tsp ground mixed spice
½ tsp ground turmeric
½ tsp cayenne pepper or chili
  powder
½ cup warm water
1 tsp salt
¼ cup ground almonds
2 hard-boiled eggs, sliced
¼ tsp paprika pepper
¼ cup chopped cilantro leaves
  (optional)

Cut each chicken joint into two, add the crushed garlic and the yogurt and stir. Cover and leave to marinate in a cool place for 2-4 hours or overnight in the refrigerator.

Heat the oil in a large pan over medium heat and fry the onions until they are golden brown. Remove them with a draining spoon and set to one side. Fry the coriander, ground pepper, ground mixed spice and turmeric for 15 seconds, then add the chicken in the same oil, with all the marinade. Fry the chicken over medium heat for 5-6 minutes until it changes color. Add the cayenne or chili powder, water, salt, and the reserved fried onions. Bring to a boil, cover the pan and simmer for about 30 minutes until the chicken is tender. Stir in the ground almonds. Garnish the curry with the sliced hard-boiled eggs and paprika, and chopped cilantro leaves, if required.

MURGHI AUR ALOO

Murghi aur aloo is a classic Parsi dish, showing the influence of this ancient Persian people on classic Indian cookery.

Serves 4-6

INGREDIENTS

2¼ pounds chicken joints, skinned
1½ tsps salt
1-inch piece of fresh root ginger, peeled and roughly chopped
4-6 cloves garlic, peeled and roughly chopped

Whole Spices
2 tsps cumin seeds
4-6 dried red chilies
2 brown cardamoms, seeds only, *or* 4 green cardamoms
6 whole cloves
2 cinnamon sticks, 2-inches long, broken up into 2-3 pieces
6 black peppercorns

1 tbsp white poppy seeds
10 raw whole cashews

4 tbsps cold water
4 tbsps ghee or sweet butter
½ cup finely chopped fresh cilantro leaves and stalks
1-2 fresh green chilies, cut into halves lengthwise, de-seeded if a mild flavor is preferred
½ tsp ground turmeric

1¼ cups warm water
½ tsp saffron strands
1 pound potatoes, peeled and quartered
⅔ cup sour cream
2-3 hard-boiled eggs, cut into quarters

Cut each chicken joint into two; separate legs from thighs and cut each breast into two pieces. Add the salt to the ginger and garlic and crush them to a pulp. Grind the whole spices, then grind the poppy seeds and cashews together. Mix the ground ingredients, including the poppy seeds and cashews, into a thick paste by adding the cold water. Break up any lumps with the back of a spoon and then set the paste aside.

Melt the ghee or butter over low heat and add the ginger and garlic paste. Cook for 2-3 minutes, stirring continuously. Add the spice paste, stir and cook for 2-3 minutes, then add the chicken and turn up the heat. Fry the chicken for 5-6 minutes until it changes color. Add the cilantro leaves, green chilies and turmeric, stir-fry for a further 2-3 minutes, then add the water. Bring to a boil and add the saffron strands, then cover and simmer for 15 minutes.

Add the potatoes to the pan and cook for a further 20 minutes or until the chicken and the potatoes are tender and the sauce is fairly thick. Beat the sour cream until smooth and stir it into the chicken. Cook, uncovered, for 6-8 minutes, stirring frequently. Arrange the chicken curry in a warmed serving dish and garnish with the hard-boiled egg quarters.

MAKKHANI MURGHI

This is a rich chicken curry in a butter sauce – it is quite an unusual dish and is certainly suitable for serving at a dinner party.

Serves 6-8

INGREDIENTS

2¼ pounds boneless chicken breast, skinned

1¼ tsps salt

1-inch piece of fresh root ginger, peeled and roughly chopped

4-6 cloves garlic, peeled and roughly chopped

⅔ cup thick plain yogurt

Juice of 1 lemon

Whole Spices

1 cinnamon stick, 2 inches long, broken up

8 green cardamoms

6 whole cloves

8-10 red chilies

6-8 white peppercorns

2 tbsps cooking oil

2 tbsps tomato paste

1 cup butter

14-ounce can tomatoes

2 cinnamon sticks, 2 inches long, broken up

⅔ cup light cream

Cut the chicken into 2 × 4-inch strips. Add the salt to the ginger and garlic and crush to a smooth pulp. Grind the whole spices. Combine the yogurt, lemon juice and the ground spices and beat until the mixture is smooth. Marinate the chicken in this mixture, cover, and leave in a cool place for 2-4 hours or overnight in the refrigerator.

Heat the oil over medium heat and add the ginger and garlic pulp. Stir-fry for 1 minute. Add the chicken and fry for 10 minutes, stirring frequently. Add the tomato paste and butter, and cook over low heat, uncovered, for 10 minutes. Remove the pan from the heat, cover and leave on one side.

Place the tomatoes and cinnamon sticks in a separate pan, bring to a boil, cover and simmer for 10 minutes. Remove the lid and cook uncovered over medium heat, until the liquid is reduced by half. Remove the pan from the heat and let the tomato mixture cool slightly, then sift the cooked tomatoes, and discard the cinnamon sticks. Add the sifted tomatoes to the chicken and place the pan over medium heat. Bring to a boil, lower the heat and cook, uncovered, for 5-6 minutes. Add the cream, stir and simmer uncovered for about 5 minutes, then serve.

SPICED ORIENTAL CHICKEN

In this unusual method of cooking chickens they are dusted with mixed spices just before serving.

Serves 6-8

INGREDIENTS
2 × 2½-3 pounds chickens, skinned
10 dried curry leaves, crumbled
¾-1 tsp cayenne pepper
2 tsps ground coriander
1 tsp ground cumin
2-3 green chilies, finely chopped
2-inch piece fresh root ginger, peeled and finely chopped
1 cinnamon stick, broken into pieces
1 tsp turmeric
5 cloves garlic, peeled and finely chopped
2 bay leaves, crumbled
2 tsps salt
2 Spanish onions, finely chopped
⅓ cup vegetable oil
1 cup coconut milk
1 tsp sugar
2 tsps lime juice

Garnish
½ tsp ground coriander
½ tsp garam masala
¼ tsp freshly ground cloves
½ tsp freshly ground cardamom seeds
½ tsp ground cinnamon

Prick the chickens all over with a fork. Mix together the curry leaves, cayenne, coriander, cumin, chilis, ginger, cinnamon, turmeric, garlic, bay leaves, salt, onions and vegetable oil. Rub the mixture all over the skinned chickens in a large bowl. Cover with plastic wrap, then leave to marinate overnight in a cool place.

Brown the chickens in the marinade in a large baking dish. Add the coconut milk, cover, and simmer gently for about 45-60 minutes until the chicken is tender. Remove the chickens from the dish and keep them warm.

Add the sugar to the cooking juices and boil to reduce the liquid a little, then stir in the lime juice and pour this sauce over the chickens.

Mix the remaining spices together and sprinkle them over the chickens just before serving.

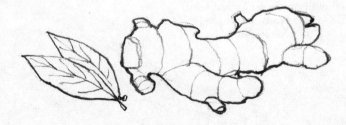

LIME AND CILANTRO CHICKEN

Cilantro and chicken make a perfect combination, especially if served with saffron scented rice.

Serves 6

INGREDIENTS

4-pound chicken, skinned (or 2 small chickens)
2 tbsps lime or lemon juice
½ tsp salt
2-3 fresh green chilies, very finely chopped
1 bunch freshly chopped cilantro leaves (with roots and lower stems removed)
¼ tsp cayenne pepper
2-inch piece fresh root ginger, peeled and finely chopped
6 tbsps plain yogurt
6 cloves garlic, peeled and crushed
2 tbsps vegetable oil
Fresh cilantro leaves and lime or lemon wedges for garnish

Prick the chicken all over with a fork. Combine the lime or lemon juice, salt and chilis in a large bowl and rub the mixture over the chicken. Set to one side while the marinade is prepared. Place the cilantro, cayenne pepper, ginger and yogurt in a bowl and mix well. Add the marinade to the chicken, coating the chicken all over. Cover the bowl with plastic wrap and leave for at least 6 hours.

Place the vegetable oil in a roasting pan with the chicken and marinade mixture. Bake the chicken in the center of a 400°F oven for 20 minutes, then lower the oven temperature to 350°F and continue baking for about 45 minutes or until the chicken is tender. The chicken should be regularly basted with the pan juices.

Skim any fat from the pan juices with a spoon. Place the chicken on a hot serving plate, spoon the sauce over and serve immediately, garnished with the fresh cilantro leaves and wedges of lime or lemon.

MURGHI BADAMI

I've always thought of chicken korma as a fairly rich, creamy dish, but this is a richer korma, cooked entirely in yogurt and cream. A succulent dish!

Serves 4-6

INGREDIENTS

2¼ pounds chicken joints, skinned
1 tsp salt
1-inch piece of fresh root ginger, peeled and chopped
3-4 cloves garlic, peeled and chopped
1 tsp freshly ground black pepper
1 tbsp lemon juice
1¼ cups thick plain yogurt
4 tbsps ghee or sweet butter
2 onions, finely sliced
6 green cardamoms, the top of each pod split open
1 tbsp ground coriander
1 tsp ground turmeric
⅔ cup light cream
¼-½ tsp chili powder
½ cup flaked almonds
1 tbsp ground almonds

Cut each chicken joint into two – separate legs from thighs and cut each breast into two pieces. Make small incisions on both sides of the chicken pieces with a sharp knife. This is to allow the spices to penetrate the flesh deeply. Add the salt to the ginger and garlic and crush to a fine pulp. Mix with the pepper and lemon juice, then rub this mixture into the chicken.

Cover and leave for 30-60 minutes. Beat the yogurt until smooth and set to one side.

Melt the ghee or butter over medium heat and fry the onions until well browned. Remove the pan from the heat and squeeze out any excess fat by pressing the onions to the side of the pan. Transfer the onions to a plate. Return the pan to the heat and add the cardamoms and coriander. Stir-fry for 30 seconds, then add the chicken. Raise the heat to medium-high and fry the chicken for 5-6 minutes until it changes color, stirring continuously. Stir in the turmeric and the yogurt. Cover the pan and simmer for 15 minutes, stirring occasionally.

Reserve 2 tbsps of the fried onions and add the rest to the chicken with the cream, chili powder and flaked almonds; stir and mix well. Cover and simmer for a further 15-20 minutes, stirring occasionally. Add the ground almonds and mix well; cover and simmer for a further 6-8 minutes. Transfer the chicken to a warmed serving dish and garnish with the remaining fried onions.

INDIAN CHICKEN

This recipe is for a spiced chicken to cook on the barbecue.
Use a 350°F oven if you prefer to cook the
chicken conventionally.

Serves 4-6

INGREDIENTS
3-pound chicken, cut into 8 joints
2¼ cups plain yogurt
2 tsps ground coriander
2 tsps paprika peper
1 tsp ground turmeric
Juice of 1 lime
1 tbsp honey
½ clove garlic, peeled and
   crushed
1 small piece fresh root ginger,
   peeled and grated

Prick the chicken all over with a fork or skewer. Combine all the remaining ingredients and spread half the mixture over the chicken, rubbing it in well. Place the chicken in a shallow dish, cover and leave for at least 4 hours or overnight in the refrigerator.

If your barbecue has adjustable shelves, place the cooking rack on the level furthest from the heat. Arrange the chicken skin side down and broil until lightly browned. Turn over and cook the second side until lightly browned. Baste frequently with the remaining marinade. Lower the grid for the last 15 minutes and cook, turning and basting frequently, until the chicken is brown and the skin is crispy. Alternatively, cook the chicken in a covered dish in a 350°F oven for 45 minutes to 1 hour, then broil for a further 15 minutes to crisp the skin.

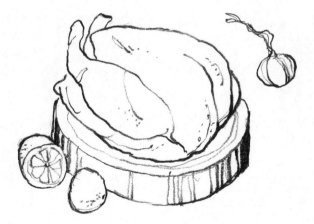

MURGHI DILKUSH

"Dilkush" sounds a little like "delicious" – a good description of this aromatic chicken curry. Use a pestle and mortar or a coffee grinder to grind the roasted spices and nuts.

Serves 6-9

INGREDIENTS
2-inch piece cinnamon stick, broken up
6 green cardamoms
6 whole cloves
1 tsp cumin seeds
2-3 dried red chilies
1 tbsp channa dhal or yellow split peas

3 tbsp raw cashews
1 tbsp white poppy seeds
2½ pounds chicken joints, skin removed
¼ cup ghee or sweet butter
2 onions, finely chopped
1-inch piece of fresh root ginger, peeled and roughly chopped
4-6 cloves garlic, peeled and roughly chopped
⅔ cup thick plain yogurt

1 tsp garam masala
⅔ cup warm water
1¼ tsps salt or to taste
1 cup finely chopped fresh cilantro leaves
1 tbsp fresh mint leaves, finely chopped *or* 1 tsp dried mint
1-2 fresh green chilies, de-seeded and coarsely chopped

Roast the whole spices and dhal over low heat until fragrant. Allow to cool, then grind. Roast the cashews and poppy seeds together in a similar way until lightly browned and grind when cool.

Cut each chicken joint into two, separate legs from thighs and cut each breast into two. Melt 2 tbsps of ghee over medium heat and fry the onions, ginger and garlic for 4-5 minutes. Squeeze out excess ghee by pressing the onions onto the side of the pan with a wooden spoon, then transfer the onions to a plate. Allow to cool slightly.

Place the yogurt in a blender or food processor and add all the roasted and ground ingredients and the fried onions. Mix until smooth. Rub this marinade into the chicken pieces and pour over any remaining marinade. Mix thoroughly and leave for 4-6 hours or overnight in the refrigerator.

Melt the remaining ghee over low heat and add the garam masala, stir-fry for 30 seconds. Add the marinated chicken, raise the heat to medium-high and fry for 5-6 minutes, stirring frequently. Add the water and salt; bring to a boil. Cover and simmer for 35-40 minutes until the chicken is tender. Raise the heat to medium, add the fresh cilantro, mint and green chilies. Stir-fry for 5 minutes, then serve with pilaf rice.

CHICKEN MOGHLAI WITH CILANTRO RELISH

A delicious dish of creamy chicken with a spicy relish or sauce. Use half parsley and half cilantro if you prefer, but the flavor of the relish will not be quite so bright.

Serves 4-6

INGREDIENTS
4 tbsps oil
3 pounds chicken pieces, skinned
1 tsp ground cardamom seeds
½ tsp ground cinnamon
1 bay leaf
4 cloves
2 onions, finely chopped
1-inch piece fresh root ginger, peeled and grated
4 cloves garlic, peeled and crushed
¼ cup ground almonds
2 tsps cumin seeds
Pinch of cayenne pepper
1¼ cups heavy cream
⅓ cup plain yogurt
2 tbsps roasted cashew nuts
2 tbsps golden raisins
Salt

Relish
3 cups fresh cilantro leaves
1 green fresh chili, de-seeded and chopped
1 tbsp lemon juice
Salt and freshly ground black pepper
Pinch of sugar
1 tbsp oil
½ tsp ground coriander

Heat the oil in a large skillet. Fry the chicken pieces on all sides until golden brown. Remove the chicken with a draining spoon and set aside. Add the cardamom, cinnamon, bay leaf and cloves to the hot oil and meat juices and fry for 30 seconds. Stir in the onions and fry until soft but not brown. Stir in the ginger, garlic, almonds, cumin and cayenne pepper. Cook gently for 2-3 minutes, then stir in the cream. Return the chicken pieces to the pan, along with any juices. Cover and simmer gently for 30-40 minutes, or until the chicken is cooked and tender.

Whilst the chicken is cooking, prepare the relish. Place the cilantro leaves, chili, lemon juice, seasonings and sugar into a blender or food processor and mix to a paste. Heat the oil and cook the ground coriander for 1 minute. Add to the blended cilantro leaves and mix thoroughly.

Just before serving, stir the yogurt, cashews and golden raisins into the chicken. Heat through just enough to plump up the sultanas, but do not let the mixture boil. Serve at once with the cilantro relish.

MURGHI MUSALLAM

This is an elegant dish of small chickens or rock Cornish game hen, stuffed and served with pilaf rice. A spiced yogurt is used to marinate the chicken and to make a sauce.

Serves 4

INGREDIENTS
2 small chickens or rock Cornish game hens, each weighing about 1 pound

Whole Spices
2 tbsps white poppy seeds
2 tbsps sesame seeds
10 black peppercorns
4 green cardamoms
2-4 dried red chilies

⅔ cup thick plain yogurt
2½ tsps salt
½ tsp ground turmeric
1 tbsp ground coriander
½ cup ghee or sweet butter
2 onions, finely sliced

2-3 cloves garlic, peeled and finely chopped
2 cinnamon sticks, 2 inches long, broken up
6 green cardamoms, the top of each pod split open
4 whole cloves
1½ cups basmati rice, washed and soaked in cold water for 30 minutes
2¼ cups water
½ tsp saffron strands
1 onion, finely chopped
2-4 cloves garlic, peeled and crushed

Remove the skin and the giblets from the chickens (or game hens). With a sharp knife, make several slits all over each chicken (do not forget the thighs and the back). Grind the whole spices and mix with the yogurt. Add 1 tsp salt, the turmeric and coriander. Rub half of this mixture into the chickens, making sure that the spices are rubbed deep into the slits. Put the chickens in a deep container, cover and leave for 1 hour.

Meanwhile cook the pilaf rice. Melt ⅓ cup of the ghee or butter over medium heat and fry the sliced onions, chopped garlic, cinnamon, cardamoms and cloves, until the onions are lightly browned. Add the rice, stir and fry for 4-5 minutes until all the moisture evaporates. Add the remaining salt, water and saffron strands. Bring to a boil, cover the pan and simmer for 12-14 minutes until the rice has absorbed all the water. Do not lift the lid or stir the rice during cooking. Remove the pan from the heat and leave it undisturbed for about 10 minutes.

Using a metal spoon, carefully transfer about a quarter of the cooked rice to a plate and allow it to cool. Keep the remaining rice covered. Stuff each chicken with as much of the cooled pilaf rice as the cavity will hold. Truss the chickens as for roasting, so that the rice stays enclosed while the stuffed chicken is being braised.

Melt the remaining ghee or butter in a cast iron or non-stick skillet. Add the chopped onion and the crushed garlic; stir-fry for 2-3 minutes. Place the chickens on the bed of onions, on their backs, along with any marinade left in the container, but not the marinade which has been reserved. Cover the pan and cook for 10 minutes; turn the chickens over, breast side down, cover and cook for a further 10 minutes. Turn the chickens on their backs again and spread the remaining marinade evenly over them. Cover the pan and cook for a further 30 minutes, turning the chickens over every 10 minutes.

Put the chickens on a warmed serving dish and spread a little sauce evenly over the breast. Spoon the remaining sauce round the chickens. Serve the remaining pilaf rice separately, reheating it if necessary.

CHICKEN LIVER MASALA

Muslims are particularly fond of liver curries – this Masala is quite hot and might be served with chapaties and relish.

Serves 4

INGREDIENTS
1 pound chicken livers
4 tbsps cooking oil
1 large onion, finely chopped
1 cinnamon stick, 2 inches long, broken up
2 medium-size potatoes, peeled and diced
1¼ tsps salt
⅓ cup warm water
3-4 cloves garlic, peeled and crushed

Spice Paste
2 tsps ground coriander
1 tsp ground cumin
1 tsp ground turmeric
½ tsp chili powder
2 tsps water

7-ounce can tomatoes
1 cup frozen peas
2-3 fresh whole green chilies
½ tsp garam masala

Clean the livers, and cut into ½-inch pieces. Heat 2 tbsps of oil over medium heat and fry the onion and cinnamon stick until the onion is soft. Add the potatoes and ¼ tsp of salt, then stir-fry the potatoes for about 2 minutes. Add the water, cover the pan and simmer until the potatoes are tender.

Meanwhile, heat the remaining oil over medium heat in a heavy-based, wide skillet. A non-stick or cast iron pan is ideal as the liver needs to be stir-fried over high heat. Add the garlic and stir-fry for 30 seconds. Mix the ground spices to a paste with the water. Add the spice paste to the pan, lower the heat and fry for about 2 minutes. Add half the tomatoes with some of the juice. Stir and cook for a further 2-3 minutes, breaking up the tomatoes with a spoon. When the mixture is fairly dry, add the livers and raise the heat to medium-high. Stir-fry the livers for 3-4 minutes. Add the remaining tomatoes and the juice, and fry for 5-6 minutes. Cover the pan and simmer for a further 6-8 minutes.

Add the cooked potatoes, peas, green chilies and the remaining salt and cook for 1-2 minutes. Lower the heat to medium and cook, uncovered, for a further 4-5 minutes. Stir in the garam masala and serve.

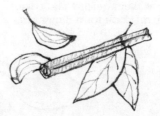

CHICKEN LIVERS WITH SPINACH

You may not immediately think of making curry with chicken livers, but this is a delicious dish of livers and spinach.

Serves 4-6

INGREDIENTS
1 pound chicken livers
1¼ tsps salt
2-3 cloves garlic, peeled
5 tbsps cooking oil
1 tsp ground turmeric
1½ tsps ground coriander
1 tsp ground cumin
¼-½ tsp chili powder
¼ tsp black mustard seeds
1 tsp cumin seeds
1 large onion, finely sliced
½ tsp garam masala
½ small red pepper, de-seeded, and cut into matchstick strips
¼ pound frozen leaf spinach (defrosted and drained) *or* 6 cups roughly chopped fresh spinach

Clean the livers, remove any tubes and cut into 1-inch pieces. Wash and drain thoroughly, and dry on paper towels. Add the salt to the garlic and crush to a pulp, using a pestle and mortar or the blade of a knife.

Heat 2 tbsps of oil over medium heat. When the oil is hot, carefully add the chicken livers. Spread them quickly and cover the pan. Cook for 6-8 minutes, stir once or twice, then remove the lid and cook off any excess liquid. Add the garlic pulp, lower the heat and stir-fry the garlic for 2-3 minutes. Add the turmeric, coriander, cumin and chili powder; stir and mix well. Cook the livers, uncovered, over low heat for 4-5 minutes, stirring occasionally.

Heat the remaining oil over medium heat in a separate pan and add the mustard seeds. As soon as they pop, add the cumin seeds followed by the onion. Stir-fry until the onion is golden brown. Add the garam masala and the red pepper and stir-fry for 1-2 minutes. Add the spinach, turn up the heat to medium-high and stir-fry the spinach for 2-3 minutes.

Add the spinach to the livers with any juices left in the pan. Lower the heat, and stir-fry the spinach and the livers for 1-2 minutes. Cook, uncovered, for a further 4-5 minutes, stirring occasionally. Serve with bread or rice.

TANDOORI CHICKEN

*One of the best known and most popular restaurant curries,
tandoori chicken really requires a tandoor oven. That
generates a particularly fierce heat, giving a lightly crusty
surface to the chicken, but leaving it moist on the inside.
Conventional ovens, give an acceptable result but the
chicken lacks the clay-cooked flavor achieved in a tandoor.*

Serves 6

INGREDIENTS
6 chicken joints
1 tsp salt
Juice of ½ lemon
½-inch piece of fresh root ginger,
  peeled and roughly chopped
2-3 small cloves of garlic, peeled
  and roughly chopped
1 fresh green chili, roughly
  chopped and de-seeded if a
  mild flavor is preferred
2 tbsps freshly chopped cilantro
  leaves
⅓ cup thick plain yogurt
1 tsp ground coriander
½ tsp ground cumin
1 tsp garam masala
¼ tsp freshly ground black
  pepper
½ tsp tandoori color, *or* a few
  drops of red food coloring
  mixed with 1 tbsp tomato paste

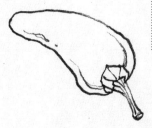

Remove the skin from the
chicken and cut each piece into
two. Make 2-3 slits in each piece,
and rub salt and lemon juice into
the chicken pieces, then set aside
for half an hour. Meanwhile, put
the ginger, garlic, green chili,
cilantro leaves and yogurt in a
blender or food processor and
mix until smooth. Add the
remaining ingredients and mix
again. Spread the marinade all
over the chicken, especially into
the slits. Cover the container and
leave the chicken to marinate for
6-8 hours or overnight in the
refrigerator.

Line a roasting pan with foil (this
will help to maintain the high
level of heat required to cook the
chicken) and arrange the chicken
pieces in it. Place the roasting
pan in the center of a 475°F oven
and bake for 25-30 minutes. Turn
the pieces over carefully as they
brown and baste with the juice in
the roasting pan as well as any
remaining marinade. Shake any
excess liquid off the chicken and
serve immediately with a salad
garnish.

TANDOORI CHICKEN MASALA

A masala is a mixture of spices. This popular chicken curry is flavored with saffron, cardamom and cinnamon.

Serves 4-6

INGREDIENTS

2¼ pounds cooked Tandoori Chicken (see recipe)
4 tbsps ghee or sweet butter
1 large onion, finely chopped
½-inch piece of fresh root ginger, peeled and crushed
2 cloves garlic, peeled and crushed
1 tsp ground cardamom seeds
1 tsp ground cinnamon
¼ tsp chili powder
1 tsp salt
⅔ cup sour cream
1 cup warm stock (made from the reserved cooking liquid from the chicken and warm water)
4 tbsps ground almonds
2 tbsps milk
½ tsp saffron strands
¼ cup toasted flaked almonds

Heat the ghee or butter over low heat and fry the onion until just soft, but not brown. Add the ginger and garlic and fry for 2 minutes, stirring constantly; then add the cardamom, cinnamon, chili powder and salt and fry for 1 minute, stirring constantly.

Beat the sour cream with a fork until smooth, adding half the stock while beating. Add this mixture to the onions and bring to a slow simmer. Add the remaining stock, cover the pan and simmer for 10 minutes. Stir the ground almonds into the mixture, then remove the pan from the heat.

Heat the milk and soak the saffron strands in it for 10-15 minutes.

Arrange the tandoori chicken in a wide shallow pan. Mix the onion and cream mixture in a blender or food processor until smooth. Pour the purée over the chicken, then pour the saffron milk and all the saffron strands into the pan. Place the pan over gentle heat and bring the liquid to a boil. Cover the pan and simmer for 15 minutes or until heated through, turning the chicken once or twice. Place the chicken in a serving dish and garnish with the toasted almonds.

MURGHI NAWABI

*Murghal cuisine, from which this recipe originates, is
delicately flavored and dressed with rich sauces. Allow the
coconut flavor to dominate the dish.*

Serves 4

INGREDIENTS
4 large chicken breasts, skinned
⅔ cup thick plain yogurt
½ tsp ground turmeric
3-4 cloves garlic, peeled and
  coarsely chopped
1-inch piece of fresh root ginger,
  peeled and roughly chopped
4-6 dried red chilies
4 tbsps ghee or sweet butter
2 large onions, finely sliced
1 tsp caraway seeds
1 tsp garam masala
1¼ tsps salt
1 cup warm water
⅓ cup flaked coconut
½ cup raw cashews
⅓ cup cold water
2 hard-boiled eggs, sliced
¼ tsp paprika pepper

Cut each chicken breast into two
pieces. Wash the chicken and dry
on paper towels. Beat the yogurt
and turmeric together until
smooth, then add to the chicken
and mix thoroughly. Cover and
leave to marinate for 4-6 hours or
overnight in the refrigerator.

Place the garlic, ginger and red
chilies in a blender or food
processor and add just enough
water to allow the ingredients to
mix until smooth. Alternatively,
crush the garlic and ginger and
finely chop the chilies.

Melt the ghee or butter over
medium heat and fry the onions
until they are brown. Remove the
pan from heat and, using a
wooden spatula, press the onions
to the side of the pan to squeeze
out excess fat. Transfer the
onions to a plate and set aside.
Return the pan to the heat. Fry
the caraway seeds and garam
masala for 30 seconds, then add
the blended garlic, ginger and
chilies. Stir briskly and add the
chicken, fried onions and salt.
Cook for 5-6 minutes, stirring
frequently and lowering the heat
as the chicken is heated through.
Add any remaining yogurt
marinade to the chicken, then
the warm water. Grind the
coconut in a coffe grinder or
pestle and mortar, and add. Bring
to a boil, cover the pan and
simmer for 30-35 minutes until
the chicken is tender and the
sauce is thick. Stir occasionally.

Meanwhile, place the cashews in
a blender or food processor, add
the cold water and mix until
smooth. Add the cashew paste to
the chicken during the last 5
minutes of cooking time. Simmer
uncovered for 4-5 minutes,
stirring frequently. Place the
chicken in a warmed serving
dish and garnish with the sliced
eggs and the paprika.

CHICKEN CHAAT

This lightly spiced, stir-fried curry may be served as a main course with salad garnish or on cocktail sticks as a drinks party savory. Serve as a main course with sliced raw onion and cucumber.

Serves 4

INGREDIENTS
1½ pounds chicken breast, skinned and boned
1 tsp salt
2-3 cloves garlic, peeled and roughly chopped
2 tbsps cooking oil
1½ tsps ground coriander
¼ tsp ground turmeric
¼-½ tsp chili powder
1½ tbsps lemon juice
2 tbsps freshly chopped cilantro leaves

Wash the chicken and dry on paper towels. Cut into 1-inch cubes. Add the salt to the garlic and crush to a smooth pulp. Heat the oil in a skillet, preferably non-stick or cast iron, over medium heat, then add the garlic and fry until it is lightly browned. Add the chicken and fry for 6-7 minutes, stirring constantly. Add the ground coriander, turmeric and chili powder. Fry for 3-4 minutes, stirring frequently. Remove from heat and stir in the lemon juice and cilantro leaves. Serve hot or cold.

SABJI MASALA MURGHI

This medium-spiced chicken curry is cooked with plenty of vegetables in the sauce, so I would suggest just serving rice or bread, pickles and raita with it.

Serves 4

INGREDIENTS
4 large chicken breasts, skinned
1 cup water
½ cup roasted cashews
4 tbsps ghee or sweet butter
1-inch piece of fresh root ginger, peeled and finely grated
4-6 cloves garlic, peeled and finely chopped

Spices
¼ tsp ground nutmeg
6 green cardamoms
1 tsp caraway seeds
4-6 dried red chilies

1¼ tsps salt
⅓ cup whole baby carrots
½ cup frozen garden peas
½ cup frozen sweetcorn
4 scallions, roughly chopped
1 small green pepper, de-seeded and finely sliced

Cut the chicken breasts into two; wash and pat dry on paper towels. Place ½ cup of the water in a blender or food processor with the cashews, and mix to a smooth paste.

Melt the ghee or butter in a large pan over medium heat and fry the ginger and garlic for 1 minute. Grind the spices in a mortar and pestle or coffee grinder. Lower the heat, add the ground spices and fry for 1 minute. Turn up the heat again, add the chicken and cook for 5-6 minutes, until the chicken changes color. Add the cashew paste, and mix thoroughly. Rinse out the blender container with the remaining water and add it to the chicken with the salt. Mix well, cover the pan and cook over low heat for 15 minutes, stirring occasionally. Add the carrots, cover and cook for a further 15 minutes; then add the peas and the sweetcorn. Cook, covered, over medium heat for 5 minutes.

Reserve half the scallions and add the rest to the chicken with the green pepper. Cook, uncovered, for 5-6 minutes, stirring frequently. Transfer the chicken to a serving dish and garnish with the reserved scallions.

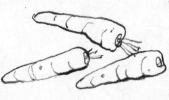
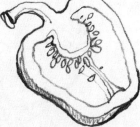

CHICKEN KOHLAPURI

The people of Kohlapur in southern India like very hot curries, flavored with lots of chilies. The quantity of chilies is scaled down slightly in this recipe – increase it if you dare!

Serves 4

INGREDIENTS
4 large chicken breasts, skinned
1 large onion, roughly chopped
2-4 cloves garlic, peeled and
  roughly chopped
1-inch piece of fresh root ginger,
  peeled and roughly chopped
⅓ cup cooking oil
1 tsp ground turmeric
2 tsps ground coriander
1½ tsps ground cumin
1-1¼ tsps chili powder

7-ounce can of tomatoes
1¼ tsps salt
¾ cup water
4-6 whole green chilies
1 tsp garam masala
2 tbsps freshly chopped cilantro
  leaves

Cut each chicken breast into two or three pieces; wash and dry on paper towels. Place the onion, garlic and ginger in a blender or food processor and mix to a smooth paste. Add a little water if necessary.

Heat the oil in a large pan over medium heat and add the onion paste. Cook for 5-6 minutes, then add the turmeric, ground coriander, cumin and chili powder. Lower the heat and cook for 4-5 minutes, stirring frequently. Add half the tomatoes, stir and cook for 2-3 minutes. Add the chicken and cook for 4-5 minutes, until the chicken changes color. Add the rest of the tomatoes, with all the juice from the can, the salt and water. Bring to a boil, cover and simmer until the chicken is tender for about 20-30 minutes. Stir occasionally to ensure that the thickened sauce does not stick to the base of the pan. Add the whole green chilies and garam masala, and cook, covered, for a further 5 minutes. Remove the pan from the heat and stir in the cilantro leaves. Season if necessary and serve.

CHICKEN WITH CHANNA DHAL

Channa dhal is available in specialist Indian shops. Yellow split peas are a suitable alternative – both go well with chicken.

Serves 6

INGREDIENTS
1 cup channa dhal or yellow split peas
6 chicken joints

Curry Paste
1 tbsp ground coriander
1 tsp ground turmeric
½ tsp cayenne pepper or chili powder
½ tsp freshly ground black pepper
1 tsp ground cinnamon
½ tsp ground nutmeg
4 tbsps water

2 tbsps cooking oil
1-inch piece of fresh root ginger, peeled and grated
3-4 cloves garlic, peeled and crushed
1 fresh green chili, finely chopped
1¼ tsps salt
2 cups warm water
3 tbsp ghee or sweet butter
1 large onion, finely sliced
2 tbsps freshly chopped cilantro leaves
1 ripe tomato, sliced

Clean and wash the channa dhal or split peas and soak them in plenty of cold water for about 2 hours. Drain well.

Cut each chicken joint into two, separating legs from thighs. Wash and pat dry on paper towels. Blend the spices for the curry paste with the water in a small bowl. Heat the oil gently in a heavy based pan and fry the ginger, garlic and green chili for 1 minute. Add the spice paste, and cook for 2-3 minutes. Add the chicken, raise the heat slightly and cook the chicken for 4-5 minutes, until it changes color. Add the dhal or split peas, and cook for a further 3-4 minutes, then stir in the salt and add the water. Bring to a boil, cover the pan and simmer until the chicken and the dhal are tender – this will take about 35-40 minutes.

Meanwhile, in a separate pan, melt the ghee or butter over medium heat and fry the onion until it is golden brown, stirring frequently. Add the onion to the chicken along with any ghee remaining in the pan. Add half the cilantro leaves and stir until all the ingredients are thoroughly mixed. Cover the pan and simmer for 10 minutes. Transfer the chicken to a serving dish and garnish with the tomatoes and remaining cilantro leaves.

CHICKEN KORMA

Chicken Korma is mild and creamy, an excellent curry to give to those who think that all Indian food is hot and spicy. I sometimes add a few tablespoons of poppy seeds for extra flavor and texture.

Serves 4

INGREDIENTS
4 chicken breasts, skinned
1-inch piece of fresh root ginger, peeled and finely grated
⅔ cup thick plain yogurt
1 small onion, roughly chopped
3-4 dried red chilies
2-4 cloves garlic, peeled and roughly chopped
½ cup cooking oil
2 cups finely sliced onions
1 tbsp ground coriander
½ tsp ground black pepper
1 tsp garam masala
1 tsp ground turmeric
⅔ cup warm water
⅓ cup flaked coconut
1¼ tsps salt
2 tbsps ground almonds
Juice of ½ lemon

Cut each chicken breast into two, then mix with the ginger and yogurt. Cover and leave to marinate in a cool place for 2-4 hours or in the refrigerator overnight.

Place the chopped onion, red chilies and garlic in a blender or food processor and mix to a smooth paste. Add a little water if necessary. Heat 5 tbsps of the oil in a large pan over medium heat and fry the sliced onions until they are golden brown. Remove the pan from the heat and, using a draining spoon, transfer the onions to another dish. Leave any remaining oil in the pan. Add the rest of the oil and return the pan to medium heat. When hot, add the ground coriander, pepper, garam masala and turmeric. Stir rapidly (take the pan off the heat if the oil is too hot) and add the chicken with the marinade. Cook for about 10 minutes, stirring frequently. Add the onion and chili mixture and continue to cook for 6-8 minutes on low heat. Stir in the water. Grind the coconut in a coffee grinder or pestle and mortar and add. Bring to a boil, stirring until the coconut is dissolved. Add the fried onion slices and salt. Lower the heat, cover the pan and simmer for about 25-30 minutes until the chicken is tender. Stir in the ground almonds, remove from the heat and add the lemon juice. Season if necessary and serve.

79

CHICKEN DO-PIAZA

"Do-piaza" literally means "cooked with twice as much onion." Be prepared to shed a tear or two while preparing this curry!

Serves 4

INGREDIENTS
4 large chicken breasts, skinned
4 large onions, roughly chopped
1-inch piece of fresh root ginger, peeled and roughly chopped
3-4 cloves garlic, peeled and roughly chopped
4 tbsps cooking oil
1 tsp ground turmeric
1 tsp ground coriander
1 tsp ground cumin
¼-½ tsp chili powder
7-ounce can tomatoes
¾ cup warm water
2 cinnamon sticks, each 2 inches long, broken up
4 green cardamoms, the top of each pod split open
4 whole cloves
2 dried bay leaves, crushed
1¼ tsp salt
2 level tbsps ghee or sweet butter
1 large onion, finely sliced
1 tbsp freshly chopped cilantro leaves

Cut each chicken breast into three pieces. Wash and dry on paper towels. Place the chopped onion, ginger and garlic in a blender or food processor and mix to a smooth paste, adding a little water if necessary.

Heat the oil in a large pan over medium heat and add the onion paste. Stir-fry for 4-5 minutes; then add the turmeric, coriander, cumin and chili powder. Fry for 4-5 minutes, stirring frequently. Add the juice from the canned tomatoes, a little at a time, to prevent the spices from sticking to the pan. Add the chicken and fry over medium heat until it has changed color. Pour in the water with the cinnamon, cardamoms, cloves, bay leaves, salt and the whole canned tomatoes. Bring to a boil. Cover and simmer until the chicken is tender and the sauce is fairly thick – about 25 minutes. Cook uncovered, if necessary, for a little longer, to thicken the sauce.

Heat the ghee or butter and fry the sliced onion for 5 minutes. Add the onions and ghee to the chicken, stir in the cilantro leaves, season and serve.

CHICKEN WITH WHOLE SPICES

This spicy chicken curry cooks quickly and does not require marinating. It is quite hot, especially if you use a whole chili.

Serves 6

INGREDIENTS
6 chicken joints, skinned
4 tbsps cooking oil
1 tsp cumin seeds
1 large onion, finely chopped
½-inch piece of fresh root ginger, peeled and finely chopped
2-4 cloves garlic, peeled and crushed or finely chopped
2-3 dried whole red chilies
2 cinnamon sticks, 2-inches long, broken up
2 brown cardamoms, the top of each pod split open
4 whole cloves
10 whole allspice berries
½ tsp ground turmeric
1 tsp paprika pepper
⅔ cup warm water
1¼ tsps salt or to taste
2 ripe tomatoes, skinned and chopped
2 whole fresh green chilies
1 tbsp ground almonds
2 tbsps freshly chopped cilantro leaves

Cut each chicken joint into two, separate legs from thighs and cut each breast in half. Heat the oil over medium heat and fry the cumin seeds until they pop; then add the onion, ginger, garlic and red chilies. Fry until the onions are soft but not brown, stirring frequently. Add the cinnamon, cardamoms, cloves and allspice, and cook for a further 30 seconds. Stir in the turmeric and paprika and then the chicken. Stir-fry over medium heat for 5-6 minutes, until the chicken is white all over. Add the water and salt and bring to a boil, then cover the pan and simmer until the chicken is tender – about 30 minutes.

Add the tomatoes, green chilies and the ground almonds. Stir and mix well, then cover the pan again and simmer for a further 6-8 minutes. Stir in half the cilantro leaves and remove the pan from the heat. Transfer the chicken to a warmed serving dish and garnish with the remaining cilantro.

DAHI MURGHI

Once the chicken has marinated in the yogurt, preferably overnight, this is quick to cook and requires little attention. Dahi Murghi is spicy yet creamy – just how I like my curries.

Serves 6

INGREDIENTS
6 chicken joints, skinned
⅔ cup thick plain yogurt
3-4 cloves garlic, peeled and
  roughly chopped
1-inch piece of fresh root ginger,
  peeled and roughly chopped
2-3 dried red chilies
½ tsp ground turmeric
1 tbsp ground coriander
4 tbsps cooking oil
1 large onion, finely sliced
2-4 fresh green chilies, whole
1 tsp salt
½ tsp garam masala
2 tbsps freshly chopped cilantro
  leaves

Cut each chicken joint into two, separate legs from thighs and cut each breast into two pieces. Wash the chicken and dry on paper towels. Place the yogurt, garlic, ginger, dried red chilies, turmeric and ground coriander in a blender or food processor and mix until smooth. Arrange the chicken in a large dish and pour the marinade over. Mix thoroughly, cover and leave to marinate for 6-8 hours, or overnight in the refrigerator.

Place the chicken and marinade in a heavy based skillet with a lid over medium heat. Stir-fry without the lid until the chicken is heated through. Cover the pan and simmer gently until the chicken is tender – about 25-30 minutes. Remove from the heat.

Heat the oil in a wide shallow pan over medium heat, add the onions and cook until browned. Add the chicken and cook uncovered for 5-6 minutes, stirring frequently. Add the whole green chilies, salt and garam masala and cook for a further 3-4 minutes. Remove the pan from the heat and stir in half the cilantro leaves. Put the chicken into a warmed serving dish and garnish with the remaining cilantro leaves.

CHICKEN TIKKA MASALA

*One of the best known chicken curries, this is moderately
spiced and served in a creamy almond sauce.*

Serves 4

INGREDIENTS
1 pound Chicken Tikka (see
recipe)
½-inch piece of fresh root ginger,
peeled and roughly chopped
2 cloves garlic, peeled and
roughly chopped
1 tsp salt
4 tbsps sweet butter
1 small onion, finely chopped
¼ tsp ground turmeric
½ tsp ground cumin
½ tsp ground coriander
½ tsp garam masala
¼-½ tsp chili powder
½ cup liquid, made up of the
reserved juice from the
Chicken Tikka and warm water
1¼ cups heavy cream
2 tbsps ground almonds

Prepare the Chicken Tikka as on
page 40. Mix together the ginger,
garlic and a ½ teaspoon of salt
and crush to a paste. Melt the
butter and fry the onion for 2-3
minutes. Add the ginger and
garlic paste and cook for 1
minute; then stir in the turmeric,
cumin, coriander, garam masala
and chili powder. Cook for 2
minutes, stirring occasionally.
Add the liquid and stir gently,
then gradually add the cream
and the remaining salt. Simmer
for 5 minutes and then add the
chicken. Lower the heat, cover
the pan and cook for 10 minutes.
Stir in the ground almonds and
simmer for a further 5-6 minutes,
before serving.

MURGHI JHAL FREZI

This is a richly spicy chicken curry, quite hot and very colorful. Serve with plain rice, Indian breads and a yogurt raita.

Serves 6

INGREDIENTS
6 chicken joints
3 large onions, finely chopped
¾ cup water
1-inch piece of fresh root ginger, peeled and grated
2-4 cloves garlic, peeled and crushed
1 tsp ground coriander
1 tsp ground cumin
1 tsp ground ajwain or caraway
½ tsp ground turmeric
½ tsp chili powder
2 cinnamon sticks, 2 inches long, broken up
2 brown cardamoms, the top of each pod split open
4 whole cloves
5 tbsps cooking oil
1¼ tsps salt
1 tbsp tomato paste
1-2 fresh green chilies, sliced lengthwise; remove the seeds for a mild flavor
2 tbsps freshly chopped cilantro leaves

Skin and cut each joint into two, separate the legs from thighs and cut each breast into two pieces. Wash the chicken and dry on paper towels. Place the chicken in a pan, add half the chopped onions, the water, ginger, garlic, coriander, cumin, ajwain, turmeric, chili powder, cinnamon, cardamoms and cloves. Bring to a boil, stir, then cover and simmer for 20-25 minutes.

Heat the oil over medium heat in a separate pan and fry the rest of the onions until they are golden brown. Add the chicken to the fried onions. Continue cooking for about 5 minutes, until the chicken is browned. Add half the spiced liquid in which the chicken was cooked, and stir-fry for 4-5 minutes until reduced. Add the rest of the liquid and fry for a further 4-5 minutes. Add salt, tomato paste, the green chilies and cilantro leaves; stir and cook over low heat for 5-6 minutes. Taste, season and serve.

MURGHI AUR PALAK

This is a classic chicken curry flavored with spinach, fennel, ground coriander and chilies – it is quite hot, so serve with plain rice and a cooling cucumber raita.

Serves 6

INGREDIENTS
6 chicken quarters, skinned
4 tbsps cooking oil
2 onions, finely chopped
1-inch piece of fresh root ginger, peeled and finely grated
2-3 cloves garlic, peeled and crushed

Curry Paste
1 tsp ground turmeric
1 tsp ground fennel
1 tsp ground coriander
½ tsp chili powder
3 tbsps water

1½ tsps salt
⅓ cup warm water
1 tbsp ghee or sweet butter
1-2 cloves garlic, peeled and finely chopped
6-8 curry leaves
½ tsp cumin seeds
½ tsp fennel seeds
1-2 dried red chilies, roughly chopped
1 pound fresh spinach *or* ½ pound frozen leaf spinach, (defrosted and drained)
4 tbsps plain yogurt
½ tsp garam masala

Cut each chicken quarter in half, separating legs from thighs and cutting each breast lengthwise into two. Heat the oil over medium heat and fry the onions, ginger and garlic until the onions are lightly browned. Lower the heat. Meanwhile, mix the curry paste ingredients in a small bowl. Add to the onion mixture and stir-fry for 4-5 minutes. Rinse out the curry paste bowl with 2 tablespoons of water and add to the pan. Stir-fry for a further 2-3 minutes. Add the chicken. Stir-fry over medium heat until the chicken changes color. Add 1 teaspoon of salt and the water, bring to a boil, then cover the pan and simmer for 15 minutes; stirring occasionally.

Melt the ghee or butter in a separate pan over medium heat. Add the garlic and curry leaves, the cumin, fennel and red chilies, then stir briskly. Wash the fresh spinach thoroughly, remove any hard stalks and add the spinach and the remaining salt. Stir-fry for 5-6 minutes. Mix the spinach and chicken together in the larger pan, bring to a boil. Cover and simmer for 20 minutes, stirring occasionally.

Mix the yogurt and garam masala together and beat until smooth. Add to the chicken and mix thoroughly. Cook, uncovered, for 6-8 minutes over medium heat, stirring frequently. Taste, add extra salt if necessary, and serve.

CHICKEN DHANSAK

A dhansak is a curry of meat or chicken cooked with lentils. Sometimes, as in this recipe, two or more types of lentils or dried peas are used. Dhansak seasoning is usually of medium heat. Tamarind concentrate is available from specialist Indian shops.

Serves 6

INGREDIENTS
6 chicken portions, skinned
1 tsp salt
1-inch piece of fresh root ginger, peeled and roughly chopped
4-6 cloves garlic, peeled and chopped
6 tbsps water

Mixed Spices
1 tsp coriander seeds
1 tsp cumin seeds
1 tsp fennel seeds
4 green cardamoms
1 cinnamon stick, 2 inches long, broken up
4-6 dried red chilies
10 black peppercorns
2 bay leaves
¼ tsp fenugreek seeds
½ tsp black mustard seeds

2 tbsps ghee or sweet butter
½ cup warm water

For the Dhal
⅓ cup toor dhal (yellow split peas)
⅓ cup masoor dhal (red lentils)
5 tbsps cooking oil
1 large onion, finely chopped
1 tsp ground turmeric
1 tsp garam masala
2¼ cups warm water
1 tsp salt
1 tsp tamarind concentrate plus 3 tbsps boiling water *or* 1½ tbsps lemon juice
1 tbsp freshly chopped cilantro leaves

Wash and dry the chicken portions and cut each portion into two. Add the salt to the ginger and garlic and crush to a pulp. Grind the spices together, then make into a paste with the ginger and garlic pulp and the 6 tbsps of water. Coat the chicken in the marinade and leave for 4-6 hours, or overnight in the refrigerator.

Melt the ghee or butter in a large skillet over medium heat and fry the chicken for 6-8 minutes, stirring frequently. Add the warm water, bring to a boil, cover and simmer for 20 minutes. Stir several times.

Meanwhile, mix together the toor and masoor dhals. Wash and drain well. Heat the oil over medium heat and fry the onions for 5 minutes, stirring frequently. Add the turmeric and garam masala, and continue cooking for 1 minute. Add the dhal, lower the heat and fry for 5 minutes, stirring frequently. Add the warm water and salt, bring to a boil. Cover and simmer the dhal for 30 minutes until soft, stirring occasionally. Press the dhal through a sifter using a metal spoon, discard the fibrous mixture left in the sifter. Pour the sifted dhal over the chicken. Cover and bring to a boil, then lower the heat and simmer for 20-25 minutes. Stir occasionally during the first half of the cooking time, and more frequently during the latter half, to ensure that the mixture does not stick to the base of the pan.

Dissolve the tamarind concentrate in 3 tbsps of boiling water. Add this to the chicken, stir and mix thoroughly. Cover and simmer for 5 minutes. Stir in the cilantro leaves and serve. If using lemon juice, simply add this at the end of the cooking time, once the chicken is cooked through and tender.

DUM KA MURGHI

A simple, delicious way of cooking chicken which is suitable for joints or a whole bird. Chicken pieces will, of course, cook more quickly.

Serves 4

INGREDIENTS
1 onion, finely chopped
2 tsps ground coriander
1 tsp chili powder
¼ tsp turmeric powder
1 tbsp tomato paste
1 tsp fresh root ginger, peeled and
2-3 cloves garlic, peeled and crushed
½ tsp salt
⅔ cup plain yogurt
3-pound chicken, cut into 8 joints
Oil

Mix the onion, coriander, chili, turmeric, tomato paste, ginger, garlic and salt with the yogurt. Rub the mixture all over the chicken pieces, then brush them with oil. Bake in a 375°F oven for 50-60 minutes, brushing with oil frequently, until the liquid has evaporated and the chicken is cooked.

To cook a whole chicken in this way, bake with the spices, wrapped in foil, for 1½-1¾ hours, then evaporate the liquid.

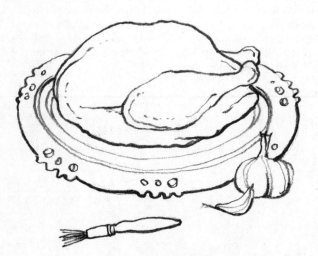

MALABARI CHICKEN

This is a rich, fruity chicken curry, delicious with pilaf rice or naan breads.

Serves 4-6

INGREDIENTS
1 large onion, chopped
4 tbsps ghee *or* 3 tbsps oil
1 inch cinnamon stick
6 green cardamoms
6 cloves
1 bay leaf
1 tsp fresh root ginger, peeled and grated
2-3 cloves garlic, peeled and crushed
3-pound chicken, cut into 8 pieces
1 tsp chili powder
1 tsp ground cumin
1 tsp ground coriander
⅔ cup plain yogurt
1 tsp salt
½ tbsp flaked coconut
2 tbsps sliced blanched almonds
2 tbsps raisins
½ cup water
2 tbsps evaporated milk
1 tbsp freshly chopped cilantro leaves
2 green chilies, chopped (optional)
1 cup pineapple chunks, fresh or canned

Fry the onion in the ghee or oil until soft, then add the cinnamon, cardamoms, cloves and bay leaf, and fry for 1 minute. Add the ginger and garlic. Stir-fry for 30 seconds, then add the chicken. Stir and cook for 2-3 minutes. Add the chili, cumin and coriander; stir well and add the yogurt and salt. Cover and cook for 10 minutes or until the yogurt is dry and the oil separates. Grind the coconut in a coffee grinder or pestle and mortar. Add the coconut, almonds, raisins and water. Cover and cook for 20-30 minutes.

Add the evaporated milk and cook for 5 minutes; then stir in the cilantro, green chilies (if used) and pineapple chunks. Cook for a further 5 minutes.

CHICKEN TOMATO

Without the spices this dish could be from almost anywhere
in the world. With the spices it is deliciously Indian!

Serves 4

INGREDIENTS
1 medium-size onion, chopped
3 tbsps oil or ghee
1 inch cinnamon stick
1 bay leaf
6 cloves
6 green cardamoms
1 inch fresh root ginger, peeled
 and sliced
4 cloves garlic, peeled and
 chopped
3-pound roasting chicken, jointed
 into 8 pieces
1 tsp chili powder
1 tsp ground cumin
1 tsp ground coriander
14-ounce can tomatoes, crushed
1 tsp salt
1 tbsp freshly chopped cilantro
 leaves
2 green chilies, halved

Fry the onion for 2 minutes in the oil or ghee. Add the cinnamon, bay leaf, cloves and cardamoms and fry for 1 minute. Add the ginger and garlic and cook for a further 30 seconds. Add the chicken pieces. Sprinkle them with chili powder, cumin and coriander and fry for 2-3 minutes, then add the crushed tomatoes. Season with salt and add the cilantro and chilies. Mix well, cover and cook for 40-45 minutes until the chicken is tender.

MEAT

Although a large number of Indians are vegetarian there are many who do eat meat, and the classic Indian cuisine contains a vast selection of recipes for meat dishes. Beef and pork are far less common than mutton and lamb and a very traditional meat is goat. Many classic meat dishes were developed for goat but are now made with lamb outside India as it is more tender and far more palatable. I can think of no other red meat which absorbs the flavors of spices as readily as lamb. Roasted, curried or as kebabs, it is my favorite meat for Indian and indeed all other meat cookery. Mutton is the meat most commonly eaten in India, but as lamb is preferred in the west most of the recipes which follow in this chapter have been adapted for lamb.

Pork, a West Coast Speciality

Pork is mainly eaten on the west coast of India, in the Christian communities around Goa. It blends well with coconut and there is an excellent recipe here for Goan Curry which makes a very pleasant change from the more common dishes of mutton and beef. Many of the meat-eating Hindus would be quite happy to eat pork but they simply don't get the opportunity to do so as pigs are raised only in a relatively small area. Muslims, however, do not eat pork as it is considered to be unclean.

Mutton and Lamb – Meat for All

The vast majority of the Indian population are Hindu and those people who do eat meat would not eat any flesh from the cow, which is considered to be sacred. With the Muslim ban on pork and most Hindus not eating beef or veal, it is safest to cook with mutton or goat in order to avoid giving offence in India, and to keep lamb for special occasions and feasts.

Not all Meat Dishes are Curries

We tend to label all Indian dishes as curries but this is about as true as saying that every American meat dish is a roast! It is simply a convenient label which we often wrongly apply. Now, having said that, I have been unable to track down an authoritative definition of a curry and must deduce that it is a mix of spices, fried and cooked with other ingredients to a sauce which may then be used to cook meat, vegetables, fish or pulses. Thus dishes that are dry cooked, broiled, baked or roasted are not curries and should not be referred to as such.

There are a few terms commonly used in Indian meat cookery that you will very quickly learn and which will help you to identify the type of dish that they describe. For example, *koftas* are meatballs and *keema* is the word for ground meat, so all keema dishes will contain ground meat – usually mutton, but beef or lamb may be used.

A Kebab by any other Name

As in all cuisines founded on a pot pourri of dishes collected from many regions, there are often a number of similar words used to describe the same basic dish. The word that confuses me most in Indian cooking is *kabab*, which I have always thought to be *kebab*. I have adopted the more familiar spelling throughout this book. Kebabs are usually pieces of meat threaded onto skewers for cooking, but occasionally kebabs are made from baked meats that are then served on cocktail sticks as nibbles or cocktail party foods.

Marinating for Tenderness and the Perfect Flavor

Many Indian dishes call for the meat to be marinated, either in a fairly dry mix of lightly roasted spices, or in a yogurt sauce flavored with spices. This custom stems back to times when the meat required this treatment to make it edible – neither goat nor mutton is renowned for its tenderness! With the better cuts of meat this custom is continued more for the benefit of the flavor of the finished dish than for the texture of the meat.

Meat that has been diced should be evenly coated in the marinade. Larger pieces and whole joints benefit from being pierced at regular intervals with a small, sharp knife, allowing the marinade to penetrate right to the bone and thus to flavor all the meat and not just the surface. Meat that has been marinated cooks slightly more quickly, and cooking times should be adjusted accordingly, especially when roasting.

MEAT DILPASAND

I love using poppy seeds in curries – they add a slightly nutty flavor and texture to the dish. I scatter a handful of poppy seeds over this curry for a garnish before serving.

Serves 4-6

INGREDIENTS

2¼ pounds lamb leg
⅔ cup thick plain yogurt
1 tsp ground turmeric
2 tbsps white poppy seeds
1-inch piece of fresh root ginger, peeled and roughly chopped
4-5 cloves garlic, peeled and roughly chopped
1-2 fresh green chilies, de-seeded if a mild flavor is preferred
4 medium onions
3 tbsps ghee or sweet butter
½ tsp chili powder
1 tsp paprika pepper
1 tbsp ground cumin
1 tsp garam masala
1 tbsp tomato paste
1¼ tsps salt
¾ cup warm water
2 tbsps flaked coconut
2 tbsps freshly chopped cilantro leaves

Trim any surplus fat from the meat, and cut the meat into 1½-inch cubes. Add the yogurt and turmeric. Mix thoroughly, cover and leave to marinate for 4-6 hours or overnight in the refrigerator.

Roast the poppy seeds without fat over gentle heat until they are a little darker – leave to cool. Place the ginger, garlic and green chilies in a blender or food processor. Chop one onion and add it to the ginger and garlic mixture. Mix until fairly smooth. Chop the remaining onions finely.

Melt the ghee or butter over medium heat and fry the onions until golden brown. Lower the heat and add the chili powder, paprika, cumin and ½ tsp garam masala. Stir-fry for 2-3 minutes, then add the blended ingredients and cook for 10-12 minutes, stirring frequently. If during this time the spices tend to stick to the base of the pan, add 1 tbsp of water when necessary. Add the meat and fry for 4-5 minutes over medium heat, stirring constantly. Stir in the tomato paste, salt and water. Bring to a boil, cover and simmer for 45 minutes or until the meat is tender. Stir occasionally during the first half of cooking, and more frequently towards the end, to ensure that the thickened gravy does not stick to the base of the pan.

Grind the coconut in a coffee grinder or pestle and mortar before use to ensure that the necessary fine texture is achieved. Grind the poppy seeds and stir into the meat with the coconut. Stir until the coconut is dissolved. Cover and simmer for 15 minutes. Stir in the cilantro leaves and the remaining garam masala, then serve immediately.

MEAT MADRAS

Madras is the major city of southern India and has given its name to the hot spicy style of curry popular throughout the south.

Serves 4-6

INGREDIENTS

6 tbsps cooking oil

2 onions, roughly chopped

1-inch piece of fresh root ginger, peeled and roughly chopped

3-4 cloves garlic, peeled and roughly chopped

4-6 dried red chilies

2 large cloves garlic, peeled and crushed

1-2 fresh green chilies, sliced lengthwise

7-ounce can tomatoes

3 tsps ground cumin

1 tsp ground coriander

½-1 tsp chili powder

1 tsp ground turmeric

2¼ pounds lamb leg or shoulder, trimmed and cut into 1½-inch cubes

¾ cup warm water

1¼ tsps salt

1 tsp garam masala

Heat 3 tbsps of oil over medium heat and fry the onions, ginger, chopped garlic and red chilies until the onions are soft, stirring frequently. Remove from the heat and let cool.

Meanwhile, heat the remaining oil over medium heat and fry the crushed garlic and green chilies until the garlic is lightly browned. Add half the tomatoes, with the juice; stir and cook for 1-2 minutes, then add the cumin, coriander, chili powder and turmeric. Lower the heat and cook for 6-8 minutes, stirring frequently. Add the meat and turn up the heat to medium-high. Stir-fry for about 5 minutes, until the meat changes color. Add the water, bring to a boil, and cover and simmer for 30 minutes.

Mix the fried onions in a blender or food processor with the remaining tomatoes until smooth. Add to the meat. Bring to a boil, add the salt and mix well. Cover the pan and simmer for a further 35-40 minutes or until the meat is tender. Stir in the garam masala and serve.

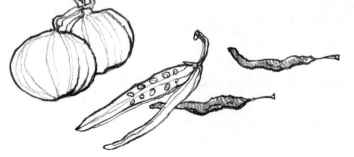

LAMB WITH MUNG BEANS

*This curry really takes three days to cook – the mung beans
require soaking on day one, the curry is cooked on day two
and left to cool, then it is actually eaten on day three, by
which time all the flavors have blended perfectly.*

Serves 6-8

Ingredients
1 cup whole mung beans,
  soaked overnight
1¼ tsps salt
1-inch piece of fresh root ginger,
  peeled and roughly chopped
2-4 cloves garlic, peeled and
  roughly chopped
1½ pounds boneless lamb leg or
  shoulder, cut into 1-inch cubes
2 cups water
1 large onion, finely chopped

Spices
2 dried red chilies
1½ tsps cumin seeds
2 tsps coriander seeds
4 whole cloves
1 cinnamon stick, 2 inches long,
  broken up
4 black peppercorns

1 tsp ground turmeric
7-ounce can tomatoes, *or* 4 ripe
  tomatoes, skinned and
  chopped
2 tbsps freshly chopped cilantro
  leaves

Soak the mung beans overnight
in plenty of cold water, then
drain well. Pulses usually contain
a certain amount of grit and
sand; make sure you clean the
beans and wash them several
times before soaking.

Add the salt to the ginger and
garlic and crush them to a
smooth pulp. Place the meat and
water in a large pan and bring to
a boil. Cover the pan and simmer
for 45 minutes. Add the mung
beans with the chopped onion.
Return to a boil, cover the pan
and simmer for a further 25
minutes. Add the ginger and
garlic pulp. Grind the spices and
add them with the turmeric and
the tomatoes. Simmer for 10
minutes, uncovered.

Remove the pan from the heat
and leave it for several hours
before serving. The longer you
let it stand, the better – overnight
is ideal. Reheat the curry, stir in
the cilantro leaves and simmer
for 5 minutes before serving.

MEAT DURBARI

Classic Indian dishes used for banquets and other great occasions tend to be quite luxurious! "Durbar" means a formal gathering, and this is a lamb dish served on such occasions.

Serves 4

INGREDIENTS
2¼ pounds lamb leg

Curry Paste:
1 tbsp mustard seeds
1 tbsp sesame seeds
2 tbsps white poppy seeds
10 black peppercorns
2-4 dried red chilies
1 bay leaf, crushed
2-inch piece of cinnamon stick, broken up
4 whole cloves
Inner seeds of 2 brown cardamoms
3 tbsps white wine vinegar

1¼ tsps salt
3-4 cloves garlic, peeled and roughly chopped
3 tbsps ghee or sweet butter
1 large onion, finely chopped
1-inch piece of fresh root ginger, peeled and finely grated
¾ cup warm water
1 tbsp tomato paste
2 fresh green chilies, slit lengthwise into halves, de-seeded if a mild flavor is preferred
2 tbsps freshly chopped cilantro leaves

Trim any excess fat from the meat, and cut the meat into 2-inch cubes. Grind the spices for the curry paste in a coffee grinder or pestle and mortar, then add the vinegar. Rub the spice paste into the meat and leave to marinate for 4-6 hours, or overnight in the refrigerator.

Add the salt to the garlic and crush to a smooth pulp. Melt the ghee or butter gently over low heat, add the onions and ginger and fry until the onions are soft. Add the garlic paste and fry for a further 2-3 minutes, stirring frequently. Add the meat and cook until all sides of the meat are sealed and brown. Add the water, bring to a boil, then cover and simmer until the meat is tender – about 30-40 minutes. Add the tomato paste, green chilies and cilantro leaves – turn up the heat to medium and cook for 3-4 minutes, stirring continuously. Remove the pan from the heat, season to taste and serve.

PASANDA BADAM CURRY

*A pasanda is a curry from the north of India, rich, creamy
and amongst my favorites!*

Serves 4-6

INGREDIENTS
2 pounds boneless lamb leg
1-inch piece of fresh root ginger,
 peeled and roughly chopped
4-6 cloves garlic, peeled and
 roughly chopped
2 fresh green chilies, de-seeded
 and roughly chopped
4 tbsps plain yogurt
4 tbsps ghee or sweet butter
3 onions, finely sliced
½ tsp ground turmeric
1 tsp ground cumin
2 tsps ground coriander
½ tsp ground nutmeg
¼-½ tsp chili powder
1 cup warm water
1¼ tsps salt
⅔ cup light cream
3 tbsps ground almonds
1 tsp garam masala or ground
 mixed spice
2 tbsps rosewater
½ tsp paprika pepper

Beat the lamb to a thickness of
¼ inch; then cut it into thin
slices, about 1½ inches long and
½ inch wide. Place the ginger,
garlic, green chilies and yogurt in
a blender or food processor and
mix until smooth. Melt the ghee
or butter over medium heat and

fry the onions until they are
lightly browned. Add the
turmeric, cumin, coriander,
nutmeg and chili powder. Lower
the heat and cook for 2-3
minutes. Stir in the meat and fry
it over high heat for 3-4 minutes
or until it changes color. Add
about 2 tbsps of the yogurt
mixture and cook for 1-2
minutes, stirring frequently.
Repeat this process until all the
yogurt mixture is used up.

Fry the meat over medium heat
for 4-5 minutes, stirring
frequently. When the fat begins
to seep through the thick spice
paste and floats on the surface,
add the water. Bring to a boil,
cover the pan and simmer for
about 1 hour until the meat is
tender, stirring occasionally.

Add the salt, cream and ground
almonds to the pasanda and let it
simmer uncovered for 5-6
minutes. Stir in the garam masala
and rosewater and remove from
the heat. Transfer the pasanda to
a warmed serving dish and
sprinkle the paprika on top.

BHOONA GOSHT

To cook this dish really well it is important to fry each ingredient over the correct heat. "Bhoona Gosht" literally means fried meat.

Serves 4-6

INGREDIENTS

2¼ pounds lamb leg or shoulder
5 tbsps cooking oil
3 large onions, finely chopped
1-inch piece of fresh root ginger, peeled and grated or finely chopped
3-4 cloves garlic, peeled and crushed
1 tsp ground turmeric
2 tsps ground cumin
1 tbsp ground coriander
½-1 tsp chili powder
1 cup warm water
1¼ tsps salt
2 ripe tomatoes, skinned and chopped; canned tomatoes may be used instead
4-5 whole fresh green chilies
1 tsp garam masala
1 tbsp freshly chopped cilantro leaves
2 small ripe tomatoes, sliced

Trim off any excess fat from the meat, then cut the meat into 1-inch cubes. Heat the oil over medium heat and add the onions, ginger and garlic. Fry until the onions are just soft; then lower the heat and add the turmeric, cumin, coriander and chili powder. Stir-fry for 2-3 minutes. Add the meat, raise the heat to medium and fry for 5 minutes, stirring frequently.

Cover the pan and cook on medium heat for about 15-20 minutes until all the liquid has disappeared. Stir frequently.

Turn the heat to high and fry the meat for 2-3 minutes; stirring continuously. Lower the heat to medium again and fry for a further 7-8 minutes, stirring frequently. The meat should now look fairly dry and the fat should have separated out. Some of the fat can be drained off at this stage, but be careful not to drain off any of the spices. Add the water and salt, bring to a boil. Cover and simmer for 50-60 minutes or until the meat is tender. Add more water if necessary. At the end of the cooking time, the thick spice paste should be clinging to the pieces of meat.

Add the chopped tomatoes and the whole green chilies. Cook for 3-4 minutes, then stir in the garam masala and half the cilantro leaves. Turn the bhoona gosht into a warmed serving dish and arrange the sliced tomatoes over the meat. Scatter the remaining cilantro leaves over the curry before serving.

SHAHI (ROYAL) KORMA

Kormas are always rich, mild and creamy but this one is extra special. "Shahi" means "royal," so this is a royal dish, perfect for a dinner party.

Serves 4-6

INGREDIENTS

2¼ pounds boneless lamb leg, trimmed and cut into 1½-inch cubes

⅔ cup thick plain yogurt

½-inch piece of fresh root ginger, peeled and grated

3-4 cloves of garlic, peeled and crushed

4 tbsps ghee or sweet butter

2 onions, finely chopped

2 tbsps coriander seeds

8 green cardamoms

10 whole black peppercorns

3-4 dried red chilies

1 tsp ground cinnamon

1 tsp ground mace

3-4 tbsps freshly chopped fresh mint, *or* 1½ tsps dried mint

½ cup ground almonds

1¼ cups warm water

½ tsp saffron strands, crushed

1½ tsps salt

½ cup raw split cashews

⅔ cup light cream

1 tbsp rosewater

Place the meat in a bowl with the yogurt, ginger and garlic. Mix thoroughly, cover the bowl and leave to marinate for 2-4 hours or overnight in the refrigerator.

Place the marinated meat, with any remaining marinade, in a heavy-based pan over medium-low heat. Bring to a slow simmer, then cover and cook the meat in its own juice for 45-50 minutes, stirring occasionally. Take the pan off the heat and remove the meat with a slotted spoon. Transfer the meat to a dish and keep hot.

Grind the whole spices, then add the cinnamon and mace. Melt the ghee over medium heat and fry the onions until they are lightly browned, then lower the heat and add the ground spices and the mint; stir-fry for 2-3 minutes. Add half of the liquid from the meat, stir and cook for 1-2 minutes. Add the ground almonds and mix thoroughly; then add the remaining liquid from the meat, stir and cook for a further 1-2 minutes. Raise the heat to medium and add the meat; stir and cook for 5-6 minutes. Add the water, saffron strands, salt and cashews. Bring to a slow boil, then cover and simmer for 20 minutes. Add the cream, stir and mix well. Simmer very slowly, uncovered, for 6-8 minutes, then stir in the rosewater and remove from the heat.

ALOO GOSHT

This potato and lamb curry can be made even more special by using sweet potatoes, giving a rich flavor.

Serves 4-6

INGREDIENTS
2¼ pounds lamb leg or shoulder
1¼ tsps salt
1-inch piece of fresh root ginger, peeled and roughly chopped
3-4 cloves garlic, peeled and roughly chopped
2 tbsps ghee or sweet butter
1 pound potatoes, peeled and cut into 1½-inch cubes
3 tbsps cooking oil
1 large onion, finely chopped
3-4 dried red chilies
2 cinnamon sticks, 2-inches long, broken up

Spice Paste
1 tbsp ground coriander
1 tsp ground allspice
1 tsp paprika
1 tsp ground turmeric
¼-½ tsp chili powder
3 tbsps water

1 tbsp tomato paste
2 brown cardamoms, the top of each pod split open
4-6 whole cloves
2 cups warm water
1 tbsp lemon juice
2 tbsps freshly chopped cilantro leaves

Trim any excess fat from the meat and cut the meat into 1½-inch cubes. Add the salt to the ginger and garlic and crush to a pulp. Melt the ghee or butter over medium heat in a non-stick or cast iron pan and fry the potatoes until they are well browned on all sides – about 10 minutes. Remove the potatoes with a slotted spoon and keep to one side. Add the oil to any ghee remaining in the pan and, when hot, fry the onion, red chilies and cinnamon sticks until the onion is soft. Add the ginger and garlic pulp, and fry for a further 2-3 minutes stirring frequently. Lower the heat and add the spice paste. Stir-fry for 3-4 minutes, then add the meat. Raise the heat to medium-high and fry for 5-6 minutes until the meat changes color, then stir in the tomato paste. Add the cardamoms, cloves and water. Bring to a boil, cover and simmer for 45-50 minutes.

Add the fried potatoes, bring to a boil again and cover and simmer for 15-20 minutes or until the potatoes are tender. Remove from the heat and add the lemon juice and cilantro leaves before serving.

MEAT VINDALOO

Vindaloo is a hot curry (too hot for me!) and the heat is accentuated by the use of vinegar in the marinade. Adjust the number of chilies if you wish.

Serves 4-6

INGREDIENTS

Whole Spices
2 tbsps coriander seeds
1 tbsp cumin seeds
6-8 dried red chilies
1 tbsp mustard seeds
½ tsp fenugreek seeds

3-4 tbsps apple cider or white wine vinegar
1 tsp ground turmeric
1-inch piece of fresh root ginger, peeled and finely grated
3-4 cloves garlic, peeled and crushed
2¼ pounds lamb shoulder or casserole beef
4 tbsps cooking oil
1 large onion, finely chopped
1-2 tsps chili powder
1 tsp paprika pepper
1¼ tsps salt
2 cups warm water
2-3 potatoes
1 tbsp freshly chopped cilantro leaves (optional)

Grind the whole spices together; then add the cider or vinegar to make a paste. Add the turmeric, ginger and garlic, and mix thoroughly. Trim any excess fat from the meat, then cut the meat into 1-inch cubes. Add the meat to the spices and mix well so that all the pieces are fully coated with the paste. Cover and leave to marinate for 4-6 hours or overnight in the refrigerator.

Place the meat in a pan over medium heat, and cook for 5 minutes. Cover the pan, and cook the meat in its own juice for 15-20 minutes, or until the liquid is reduced to a thick paste. Stir occasionally during this time to ensure that the meat does not stick to the base of the pan. Remove from the heat and put to one side.

Heat the oil in a large pan over medium heat and fry the onions until they are soft, then add the meat and fry for 6-8 minutes, stirring frequently. Add the chili powder, paprika and salt. Stir-fry for a further 2-3 minutes, then add the water. Bring to a boil. Cover and simmer for 40-45 minutes or until the meat is nearly tender (beef will take longer to cook, and you may need to add more water during cooking).

Meanwhile, peel and wash the potatoes. Cut them into approximately 1½-inch cubes. Add to the meat and bring to a boil again. Cover the pan and simmer for 15-20 minutes until the potatoes are cooked. Turn the vindaloo onto a warmed serving dish and garnish with the cilantro leaves if wished.

NAWABI KHEEMA PILAU (GROUND LAMB PILAF)

This mouthwatering pilaf is unusual as it includes ground lamb in the rice. Serve with a vegetable curry of your choice.

Serves 4-6

INGREDIENTS
1½ cups basmati rice
5 tbsps ghee or sweet butter
3 tbps golden raisins
3 tbsps raw cashews, split into halves
2 tbsps milk
1 tsp saffron strands
6 green cardamoms, the top of each pod split open
4 whole cloves
1 tsp cumin seeds
2 bay leaves, crushed
1-inch piece of fresh root ginger, peeled and grated
2-3 cloves garlic, peeled and crushed
1-2 fresh green chilies, finely chopped, de-seeded if a mild flavor is preferred
1 tsp ground nutmeg
1 tsp ground cinnamon
1 tsp ground cumin
1 tbsp ground coriander
1 pound lean ground lamb
2¼ cups water
1¼ tsps salt
⅔ cup light cream
2 tbsps rosewater
2 hard-boiled eggs, sliced

Wash and soak the basmati rice in cold water for 30 minutes, then drain. Melt 1 tbsp of the ghee or butter over low heat and fry the golden raisins until they swell, then remove them with a slotted spoon and put to one side. Fry the cashews in the same fat until they are lightly browned, then remove them with a slotted spoon and put to one side.

Boil the milk, add the saffron strands and leave until required. Melt the remaining 4 tbsps ghee or butter gently over low heat and fry the cardamoms, cloves, cumin seeds and bay leaves for 1 minute. Add the ginger, garlic and green chilies and stir-fry for 30 seconds. Add the nutmeg, ground cinnamon, cumin and coriander and fry for 1 minute. Stir in the ground lamb and raise the heat to medium. Stir-fry the meat until all the liquid dries up and it is lightly browned. This will take about 5 minutes. Add the rice, stir-fry for a further 5 minutes, then add the water, salt, cream, steeped saffron and milk. Stir and mix well. Bring the liquid to a boil, cover the pan and simmer for 12-15 minutes without lifting the lid. Remove the pan from the heat and leave it undisturbed for a further 10-15 minutes.

Add half the nuts and golden raisins to the rice, then sprinkle the rosewater over the top. Using a fork, mix gently into the rice. Turn the pilaf into a warmed serving dish. Garnish with the remaining nuts and golden raisins and the sliced hard-boiled eggs.

MEAT DILRUBA

This delicious meat curry is in a class of its own. It is cooked in two stages, making it easy to get much of the preparation and cooking out of the way in advance.

Serves 4-6

INGREDIENTS

2¼ pounds boneless lamb leg
1¼ tsps salt
½-inch piece of fresh root ginger, peeled and finely chopped
3-4 cloves garlic, peeled and finely chopped
1 tsp ground turmeric
⅔ cup thick plain yogurt
1 large onion, finely sliced
3-4 dried red chilies, roughly chopped
⅔ cup water

1 tbsp white poppy seeds
1 tsp fenugreek seeds

⅔ cup flaked coconut

2 tbsps ghee or sweet butter
2 tbsps ground coriander
⅔ cup milk
4-5 tbsps freshly chopped cilantro leaves
1 fresh green chili, cut lengthwise into thin strips, de-seeded if preferred

Trim any excess fat from the meat, then cut the meat into 1-inch cubes. Place the salt ginger and garlic in a pestle and mortar and crush them to a pulp. Alternatively, use a chopping board and crush them with the end of a wooden rolling pin. Mix together the ginger and garlic pulp, the turmeric and the yogurt and beat until the mixture is smooth. Add this to the meat. Mix thoroughly, cover and leave to marinate for 4-6 hours or overnight in the refrigerator.

Place the marinated meat in a heavy based pan; add the onion, red chilies and the water. Bring to a slow simmer over gentle heat. Cover the pan and simmer for 50-60 minutes or until the meat is tender. Remove from the heat.

Grind the poppy and fenugreek seeds, then grind the flaked coconut separately. Melt the ghee over medium heat and add the ground coriander; stir-fry for 30 seconds. Add the ground poppy and fenugreek seeds and fry until the mixture is lightly browned, stirring constantly. Remove the meat from the cooking liquor and add it to the poppy and fenugreek mixture. Stir-fry over medium-high heat for 6-7 minutes until all the moisture evaporates. Add the ground coconut and fry for 2 minutes, then add the milk and the liquid in which the meat was cooked. Stir and mix thoroughly. Cook, uncovered, over low heat for 4-5 minutes, stirring frequently. Stir in the cilantro leaves and the green chili, remove from the heat and serve.

MEAT MAHARAJA

*A rich lamb curry with poppy seeds and ground almonds –
fit for the Maharajas.*

Serves 4-6

INGREDIENTS

4 tbsps ghee or sweet butter
2 large onions, roughly chopped
1-inch piece of fresh root ginger,
  peeled and roughly chopped
4-6 cloves garlic, peeled and
  roughly chopped
1 fresh green chili, de-seeded
  and chopped
1-2 dried red chilies, chopped
⅔ cup thick plain yogurt
1 tsp black cumin seeds or
  caraway seeds
3 tsps ground coriander
1 tsp garam masala
1 tsp ground turmeric
¼ tsp ground black pepper
2 tbsps white poppy seeds,
  ground
2¼ pounds boneless lamb leg,
  cut into 1-inch cubes
¾ cup warm water
1¼ tsps salt
2 tbsps ground almonds
2 tbsps freshly chopped cilantro
  leaves
1 tbsp lemon juice
3 tbsps lightly crushed unsalted
  pistachio nuts

Melt 2 tbsps of the ghee over
medium heat and fry the onions,
ginger, garlic, green and red
chilies until the onions are just
soft. Remove from the heat and
let cool slightly. Place the yogurt
in a blender or food processor,
add the onion mixture and mix
to a paste. Set to one side.

Heat the remaining ghee or
butter over low heat (do not
overheat ghee) and add the
black cumin or caraway seeds.
Mix the ground spices together
and add them with the ground
poppy seeds. Stir-fry for 1
minute, then add the meat.
Increase the heat to medium-
high; stir-fry for 4-5 minutes until
the meat changes color. Cover
the pan and let the meat cook in
its own juices for 15 minutes. Stir
occasionally.

Add the yogurt and onion
mixture and mix thoroughly.
Rinse out the blender container
with the warm water and add
this to the meat. Stir in the salt
and bring to a boil, cover the
pan and simmer for about 40
minutes until the meat is tender.
Stir occasionally during the first
half of the cooking time, and
more frequently towards the end
to ensure that the thickened
sauce does not stick to the base
of the pan. Stir in the ground
almonds and half the cilantro
leaves. Cook, uncovered, for 2-3
minutes. Remove the pan from
the heat and add the lemon juice,
then mix well. Garnish with the
remaining cilantro leaves and
scatter the crushed pistachio nuts
over the curry.

KOFTA (MEATBALL) CURRY

Meatballs are popular throughout India. I always make them with finely ground meat as they stay together better than those made with coarsely ground meat.

Serves 4

INGREDIENTS
For the Koftas
1 pound lean ground lamb
2 cloves garlic, peeled and chopped
½-inch piece of fresh root ginger, peeled and roughly chopped
1 small onion, roughly chopped
4 tbsps water
1 fresh green chili, de-seeded and chopped
2 tbsps freshly chopped cilantro leaves
1 tbsp freshly chopped mint leaves
1 tsp salt

For the Sauce or Gravy
5 tbsps cooking oil
2 onions, finely chopped
½-inch piece of fresh root ginger, peeled and grated
2 cloves garlic, peeled and crushed
2 tsps ground coriander
1½ tsps ground cumin
½ tsp ground turmeric
¼-½ tsp chili powder
7-ounce can tomatoes
⅔ cup warm water
½ tsp salt
2 brown cardamom pods, opened
4 whole cloves
2-inch piece cinnamon stick, broken up
2 bay leaves, crushed
2 tbsps thick plain yogurt
2 tbsps ground almonds
1 tbsp freshly chopped cilantro leaves

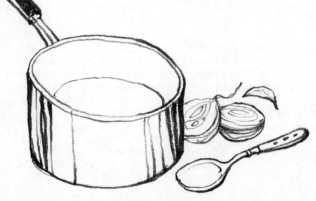

Place half the meat with the garlic, ginger, onion and water in a pan over medium heat. Bring slowly to a boil, then cover and simmer for 30-35 minutes until all liquid evaporates. Cook uncovered if necessary to dry out any excess liquid. Combine the cooked meat with the rest of the kofta ingredients, including the raw meat. Place the mixture into a blender or food processor and mix until smooth. Chill the mixture for 30 minutes.

Divide the meat mixture into approximately 20 pieces, each slightly bigger than a walnut. Roll them between your hands to make neat round koftas.

Heat the oil for the sauce over medium heat and fry the onions until they are just soft. Add the ginger and garlic and fry for 1 minute, then add the coriander, cumin, turmeric and chili powder and stir quickly. Add one tomato at a time to the spice mixture with a little of the juice, stirring until the mixture begins to look dry. Add the water, salt, cardamoms, cloves, cinnamon and bay leaves. Stir once and add the koftas. Bring to a boil, cover and simmer for 5 minutes.

Beat the yogurt with a fork until smooth, add the ground almonds and beat again. Stir gently into the curry. Cover and simmer until the koftas are firm. Stir the curry gently, cover again, and simmer for a further 10-15 minutes, stirring occasionally to ensure that the thickened sauce or gravy does not stick to the pan. Stir in half the cilantro leaves and serve.

SIKANDARI RAAN (ROASTED SPICED LAMB AND POTATOES)

This is a wonderful way to roast a lamb leg. The meat is marinated for 48 hours before being cooked, coated with a yogurt and cashew nut paste.

Serves 6-8

INGREDIENTS
3½-4 pounds lamb leg

1¼ cups thick plain yogurt
1-inch piece of fresh root ginger, peeled and roughly chopped
4-6 cloves garlic, peeled and roughly chopped
1 onion, roughly chopped
1 fresh green chili
2 tbsps freshly chopped mint *or* 1 tsp dried mint

1 tbsp ground coriander
1 tsp ground cumin

1 tsp garam masala
1 tsp ground turmeric
1¼ tsps salt or to taste

2 tbsps white poppy seeds
1 tbsp sesame seeds
2 tbsps flaked coconut

2 tbsps ghee or sweet butter
1 pound potatoes, peeled and halved

⅔ cup thick plain yogurt
⅓ cup raw cashews
⅓ cup seedless raisins, soaked in a little warm water for 30 minutes

Trim as much fat as possible from the meat. Make deep incisions from top to bottom at about ¼-inch intervals. These incisions should be as deep as possible, almost down to the bone. Turn the leg over and repeat the process. Mix the yogurt with the ginger, garlic, onion, green chili and mint in a Blender or food processor, until smooth. Add the ground spices and salt and blend again. Grind the poppy and sesame seeds with the coconut and add this to the spiced yogurt. Rub the mixture over the lamb, forcing it into the incisions. Place in a covered container and leave to marinate in the refrigerator for 48 hours. Turn the meat every 12 hours.

Place the leg of lamb in a roasting pan, melt the ghee or butter and pour it over the meat. Cover the meat with foil or use a covered roasting pan. Cook in the center of the oven for 20 minutes. Lower the temperature to 375°F and cook for a further 30 minutes. Add the potatoes and spoon some of the spiced yogurt over them as well as over the meat. Cover and cook for a further 35-40 minutes, basting the meat and the potatoes occasionally with more of the yogurt.

Mix the remaining yogurt with the cashews and raisins in a Blender or food processor until smooth. Pour the blended nut mixture over the meat. Cover and return the meat to the oven for about 30 minutes, basting the meat and the potatoes as before. Transfer the meat to a warmed serving dish and arrange the potatoes around it. Spoon any remaining liquid over the meat and the potatoes. Serve the meat cut into chunky pieces rather than thin slices.

ROGAN JOSH

Rogan Josh is spicy yet creamy, a rich blend of lamb, tomatoes and seasonings. It is one of my favorite restaurant curries.

Serves 4-6

INGREDIENTS

3 tbsps ghee or sweet butter
2¼ pounds boneless lamb leg, cut into 1½-inch cubes
1 tbsp ground cumin
1 tbsp ground coriander
1 tsp ground turmeric
1 tsp chili powder
1-inch piece of fresh root ginger, peeled and grated
2-4 cloves garlic, peeled and crushed
2 medium onions, finely sliced
14-ounce can tomatoes, chopped or whole
1 tbsp tomato paste
½ cup warm water
1¼ tsps salt
6 tbsps heavy cream
2 tsps garam masala
2 tbsps freshly chopped cilantro leaves

Melt 2 tbsps of the ghee or butter over medium heat and fry the meat in 2-3 batches until it changes color. Remove each batch from the pan with a slotted spoon and put to one side. Turn the heat down as low as possible and then add the cumin, coriander, turmeric, chili powder, ginger and garlic. Stir-fry for 30 seconds. Raise the heat again to medium and add the meat with all its juices. Stir-fry for 3-4 minutes, then add the onions. Fry for 5-6 minutes, stirring frequently, then add the tomatoes and tomato paste and cook for 2-3 minutes. Add the water and salt, bring to a boil, cover and simmer until the meat is tender – for about 60 minutes. Stir in the cream and remove the pan from the heat.

In a separate pan melt the remaining ghee over medium heat and add the garam masala, stir briskly and add to the meat. Transfer a little meat gravy to the pan in which the garam masala was fried. Stir thoroughly to ensure that any remaining garam masala and ghee mixture is fully incorporated into the gravy and add this to the meat. Mix well. Stir in the cilantro leaves, then serve.

KASHMIRI LAMB KEBABS

These kebabs are easy to prepare and will benefit from as long a marinade as you can give them – the longer the marinade, the tastier the meat. Cook the kebabs on the barbecue in the summer.

Serves 4

INGREDIENTS

1½ pounds boneless lamb, shoulder or leg
2 tbsps oil
1 clove garlic, peeled and crushed
1 tbsp ground cumin
1 tsp turmeric
1 tsp fresh root ginger, peeled and grated
A few freshly chopped cilantro or parsley leaves
Salt and freshly ground black pepper
1 red pepper, de-seeded and cut in 1-inch pieces
1 small onion, cut in rings

Cut the lamb into 1-inch cubes. Heat the oil and cook the garlic, cumin, turmeric and ginger for 1 minute; then add the cilantro, salt and pepper. Let cool, then rub the spice mixture over the meat. Leave covered in the refrigerator for several hours.

Thread the meat onto skewers, alternating it with the pepper pieces. Cook for about 10 minutes under a broiler, turning frequently. During the last 5 minutes, thread sliced onion rings around the meat. Continue cooking until the onion is cooked and lightly browned and the meat is cooked to your taste.

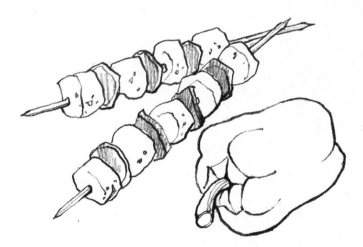

DAM KE KÁBAB (BAKED KEBAB)

This is so simple to make and utterly delicious! The spiced meat is baked and then cut into pieces. Serve as a main course or, cut into small pieces and threaded onto cocktail sticks, as a savory appetizer.

Serves 4

INGREDIENTS

1 pound lean ground beef or lamb
1 tsp fresh root ginger, peeled and grated
2-3 cloves garlic, peeled and crushed
2 green chilies, ground or finely chopped
2 tsps garam masala
⅔ cup plain yogurt
¼ tsp meat tenderizer (optional)
1 tbsp freshly chopped cilantro leaves
1 tsp chili powder
2 eggs, lightly beaten
1 onion, thinly sliced and fried until crispy
Salt
Oil
2 green chilies, chopped
Juice of 1 lemon

Mix together the meat, ginger, garlic, ground chili, garam masala, yogurt, meat tenderizer (if used), half the finely chopped cilantro, the chili powder, eggs and crisply fried onions. Stir well and season with salt. Spread the mixture over a well greased baking sheet – it should be ½ inch thick. Brush with oil and bake in a 350°F oven for 20 minutes. Lower the temperature to 300°F and cook for a further 20-30 minutes, or until any liquid has evaporated. Cut the meat into 2-inch squares. Garnish with the remaining chopped chilies and fresh cilantro. Sprinkle with lemon juice before serving.

SAVORY MEAT & EGGS

The eggs are baked on a bed of spiced ground meat to provide an economical and filling family dish. I always lightly prick the egg yolks before baking, which prevents them from splitting.

Serves 4-6

INGREDIENTS
4 tbsps cooking oil
1 large onion, roughly chopped
1-inch piece of fresh root ginger, peeled and roughly chopped
4-6 cloves garlic, peeled and roughly chopped
⅔ cup thick plain yogurt
1 tsp cumin seeds
1 tsp ground turmeric
1 tsp ground coriander
1 pound lean ground beef or lamb
1 tsp paprika pepper
1¼ cup warm water
1 tsp salt
1 tbsp tomato paste
½ tsp garam masala
2 tbsps freshly chopped cilantro leaves
4-6 small eggs (1 per person)

Heat 2 tbsps of oil over medium heat and fry the onion, ginger and garlic for 3-4 minutes, stirring frequently. Remove from the heat and let cool slightly. Place the yogurt and fried onion mixture in a blender or food processor and mix until smooth. Set aside.

Heat the remaining oil and fry the cumin seeds until they pop. Remove the pan from the heat and add the turmeric and coriander. Stir and mix thoroughly. Adding the spices away from the heat prevents them from burning. Place the pan back on the heat and add the meat. Fry over medium heat until the meat is lightly browned and completely dry. Add the paprika, water and salt, bring to a boil, and cover and simmer for 15 minutes. Stir occasionally.

Add the blended yogurt and onion and the tomato paste. Return to a boil. Cover and simmer for a further 15 minutes, stirring occasionally. Stir in the garam masala and the cilantro leaves, then remove the pan from the heat. Turn the meat into a baking dish, making a hollow for each egg to be used, about 1 inch apart. Break an egg into each hollow; do not worry about the egg white spilling over. Bake in the center of a 375°F oven for 30 minutes or until the eggs are set. Bake for a few minutes longer if you like the yolks hard. Garnish with the remaining cilantro leaves before serving.

KHEEMA-PALAK
(MEAT WITH SPINACH)

I have only recently realized that ground meat is seldom cooked by itself in India – most classic curries made with it include a second main ingredient, either a vegetable or eggs. One of the most popular vegetables for curry – spinach – is used in this dish.

Serves 4-6

INGREDIENTS
4 tbsps cooking oil
½ tsp black mustard seeds
1 tsp cumin seeds
1 fresh green chili, finely chopped, de-seeded if a mild flavor is preferred
1-inch piece of fresh root ginger, peeled and finely grated
6 cloves garlic, peeled and crushed
1 pound lean ground beef or lamb
1 large onion, finely sliced
2 cinnamon sticks, 2 inches long, broken up
½ tsp ground turmeric
1 tbsp ground cumin
½ tsp ground black pepper
¾ pound fresh spinach leaves, chopped *or* ½ pound frozen spinach, defrosted and drained
1 tsp salt
7-ounce can tomatoes, drained and chopped, *or* 3-4 ripe tomatoes, skinned and chopped
1 tsp garam masala

Heat 2 tbsps of oil in a wide shallow pan over medium heat and fry the mustard seeds until they crackle. Add the cumin seeds, green chili, ginger and half the garlic. Stir-fry for 30 seconds. Add the meat and cook until all the liquid evaporates – this will take 8-10 minutes. Remove the pan from the heat and set aside.

Heat the remaining oil in a separate pan over medium heat and stir in the remaining garlic. Add the onion and cinnamon sticks and fry until the onion is lightly browned, stirring frequently. Lower the heat and add the turmeric, cumin and black pepper. Stir-fry for 1 minute, then add the spinach and mix thoroughly. Add the meat and stir until the spinach and the meat are thoroughly mixed. Cover the pan and simmer for 15 minutes. Turn up the heat slightly, add the salt and the tomatoes, and stir and cook for 2-3 minutes. Add the garam masala, and cook for a further 2-3 minutes. Remove the pan from the heat, add a little extra salt and pepper if necessary, and serve.

KHEEMA SHAHZADA

"Kheema" is the Indian word for ground meat. The best meat for curries should be lean but quite coarse – ground steak is really too fine.

Serves 4

INGREDIENTS

6 tbsps ghee or sweet butter
1 large onion, roughly chopped
1-inch piece of fresh root ginger, peeled and roughly chopped
2-4 cloves garlic, peeled and roughly chopped

1 cinnamon stick, 2 inches long, broken up
4 green cardamoms
4 whole cloves
4-6 dried red chilies
1 tbsp coriander seeds

1 tbsp white poppy seeds
1 tbsp sesame seeds

1 pound lean ground beef or lamb
½ tsp ground turmeric
1 tsp salt
⅓ cup raw cashews, split into halves
1¼ cups warm water
1½ cups milk
2 hard-boiled eggs, quartered lengthwise
Few sprigs of fresh cilantro leaves

Melt half the ghee or butter over medium heat and fry the onion, ginger and garlic until the onion is soft. Squeeze out any excess fat by pressing the fried ingredients onto the side of the pan with a wooden spatula, then transfer them to a plate and let cool. Grind the two separate groups of spices and seeds. Add the remaining ghee or butter to the pan and fry the ground spices and seeds for 1 minute, stirring constantly. Add the meat and fry for about 10 minutes, stirring frequently, until all the liquid evaporates; then add the turmeric and stir-fry for 30 seconds. Stir in the salt, cashews and water, then bring to a boil. Cover the pan and cook over low heat for 15 minutes, stirring occasionally.

Meanwhile, pour the milk into a blender or food processor and add the fried onion, garlic and ginger. Mix until smooth and stir into the meat. Return to a boil, cover the pan and simmer for 10-15 minutes or until the sauce is thick. Transfer the meat to a warmed serving dish and garnish with the hard-boiled eggs and cilantro leaves.

KHEEMA MATTAR (CURRIED MEAT & PEAS)

"Keema" means "ground meat," and "mattar" means "peas," so this might sound like a typical curried ground meat dish. Not so – the spices and ground almonds turn it into a delicious curry.

Serves 4

INGREDIENTS

- 6 tbsp cooking oil
- 1 tsp cumin seeds
- 2 dried red chilies
- 1 pound lean ground beef or lamb
- 1 large onion, finely chopped
- 1-inch piece of fresh root ginger, peeled and finely grated
- 4 cloves garlic, peeled and crushed
- ½ tsp ground turmeric
- 2 tsps ground coriander
- 1½ tsps ground cumin
- ½ tsp chili powder
- 7-ounce can tomatoes, *or* 3-4 fresh tomatoes, skinned and chopped
- 1 tsp salt
- 1 tbsp plain yogurt
- ¾ cup warm water
- 1 cup fresh shucked or frozen peas
- 1 tbsp ground almonds
- ½ tsp garam masala
- 2 hard-boiled eggs, sliced
- 2 tbsps freshly chopped cilantro leaves

Heat 1 tbsp of oil over medium heat and add the cumin seeds. As soon as they pop, add the red chilies and then the meat. Stir and cook until the meat is evenly browned. Meanwhile, heat the remaining oil in a large pan over medium heat and add the onion. Fry until the onion is soft, then add the ginger and garlic and cook for a further 2-3 minutes. Stir in the turmeric and then the coriander, cumin and chili powder. Add the tomatoes with all the juice; stir and cook for a further 3-4 minutes. Add the browned meat and cook for 6-8 minutes, stirring frequently. Stir in the salt and water and then the yogurt. Cover the pan and simmer for 20 minutes.

Add the peas and simmer for a further 10 minutes. If using fresh peas, boil them until tender before adding to the meat. Stir in the ground almonds and simmer for 2-3 minutes, then remove the pan from the heat and stir in the garam masala. Transfer to a warmed serving dish and arrange the sliced eggs on top. Garnish with the cilantro leaves.

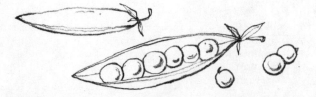

KOFTA (MEATBALL) BHOONA

A curry of meatballs will always have the word "kofta" in its title. You only need a tiny piece of root ginger for this recipe – ¼ inch is plenty.

Serves 4-6

INGREDIENTS

1 pound fine lean ground beef or lamb
1 large clove of garlic, peeled and crushed
1 tsp garam masala
1-2 fresh green chilies, de-seeded and finely chopped
2 tbsps fresh chopped cilantro leaves
1½ tsps salt
3 tbsps cooking oil
1 large onion, finely chopped
Small piece of fresh root ginger, peeled and grated
2 tsps ground coriander
1 tsp ground cumin

Spice Paste
½-1 tsp chili powder
2 cloves garlic, peeled and crushed
½ tsp ground turmeric
2 tbsps tomato paste
½ cup cold water

1 cup warm water
½ cup frozen peas
¼ tsp garam masala
2 tbsps freshly chopped cilantro leaves

Place the ground meat in a large bowl and add the garlic, garam masala, green chilies, 1 tsp salt and the cilantro leaves. Mix the ingredients thoroughly and knead the mixture until it is smooth. Divide it into about 28-30 marble-sized balls (koftas), rolling them between the palms of your hands.

Heat the oil over medium heat, preferably in a non-stick or cast iron pan, and fry the koftas in 2-3 batches. Turn the koftas as they brown and, when they are brown all over, remove them with a slotted spoon and drain on paper towels. In the same oil, fry the onion and ginger until the onion is golden brown, stirring frequently. Lower the heat and add the ground coriander. Fry for 30 seconds, then add the ground cumin and fry for a further 30 seconds. Raise the heat to medium and add 2 tbsps of the spice paste. Stir-fry until it dries up. Repeat the process until all the spice paste is used up. Add the warm water and the remaining salt and bring to a boil, then turn down the heat, add the koftas, cover the pan and simmer for 10 minutes.

Raise the heat to medium again, and bring the bhoona to a boil. Stir and cook for 4-5 minutes. Add the peas and the garam masala and continue to cook, uncovered, until the sauce is fairly thick, stirring frequently. Stir in the cilantro leaves, add a little more salt if necessary and serve.

KHEEMA-SALI MATTAR

The Parsees, ancient Persians, settled in India and contributed some wonderful dishes to the classic cuisine of their adopted country. Some of my favorite curries are, like this rich dish, Parsi in origin. Parsi dishes are often garnished with fried potato sticks.

Serves 4-6

INGREDIENTS

5 tbsps cooking oil
1 tsp cumin seeds
1 large onion, finely chopped
½-inch piece of fresh root ginger, peeled and finely grated
3-4 cloves garlic, peeled and crushed
½ tsp ground turmeric
1 tsp ground cinnamon
½ tsp ground nutmeg
1 tsp ground mixed spice
2 tsps ground coriander
½ tsp chili powder
1 pound lean coarse ground beef or lamb
7-ounce can tomatoes
1 tsp salt
⅔ cup warm water
2 tbsps plain yogurt
1½ cups frozen peas or shucked fresh peas, boiled until tender
2 tbsps freshly chopped cilantro leaves
2 tbsps ghee or sweet butter
3 medium potatoes, peeled and cut into matchstick strips
¼ tsp salt
¼ tsp chili powder

Heat the oil over medium heat and fry the cumin seeds until they pop. Add the onion, ginger and garlic and fry until the onion is golden brown. Add the turmeric, cinnamon, nutmeg, mixed spice, coriander and chili powder. Stir-fry on low heat for 2-3 minutes. Stir in the meat and fry until the meat is brown and all the liquid has evaporated. Add the tomatoes and cook for 2-3 minutes, stirring frequently, then add the salt and water. Bring to a boil, cover and cook on low heat for 15-20 minutes.

Beat the yogurt until it is smooth and add it to the meat with the peas. Return to a boil, cover and simmer for 5 minutes. Stir in half the cilantro leaves and remove the pan from the heat.

Melt the ghee or butter over medium heat in a non-stick or cast iron pan and fry the potato sticks in a single layer until they are well browned and tender. Lower the heat as the potato starts to cook. You will need to do this in 2-3 batches. Drain the potato sticks on paper towels. Season the potato sticks with the salt and chili powder. Place the meat in the middle of a serving dish and arrange the potato sticks around it. Garnish with the remaining cilantro leaves.

CAULIFLOWER SURPRISE

This doesn't sound like an authentic name for a classic Indian recipe! However, it is an unusual and imaginative way of serving cauliflower, stuffed with ground beef or lamb.

Serves 4

INGREDIENTS
1 cauliflower
4 tbsps cooking oil
1 tsp cumin seeds
1 large onion, finely chopped
1-inch piece of fresh root ginger, peeled and grated
3-4 cloves garlic, peeled and crushed
1 pound lean ground beef or lamb
1 tsp ground turmeric
1 tbsp ground coriander
1 tsp ground cinnamon
1 tsp ground cardamom seeds
½ tsp chili powder
7-ounce can tomatoes, drained
1 tsp salt
¼ tsp black mustard seeds
½ tsp cumin seeds
8-10 curry leaves

To Garnish
2 small tomatoes, quartered
1 tbsp freshly chopped cilantro leaves

Blanch the whole cauliflower in boiling salted water, then drain and cool. Heat 3 tbsps of oil over medium heat and add the cumin seeds. As soon as the seeds start popping, add the onion and fry for 3-4 minutes, stirring frequently. Add the ginger and garlic, stir-fry for 1 minute. Add the meat. Turn the heat up slightly. Stir-fry the meat until it is crumbly and all the liquid has evaporated. Lower the heat and add the turmeric, coriander, cinnamon, cardamom and chili powder. Stir-fry for 3-4 minutes until the spices are well blended. Add the tomatoes and salt and cook, stirring continuously, for 1-2 minutes. Cover the pan and simmer for a further 10-15 minutes. Remove the pan from the heat and let to cool.

Place the cauliflower on a board, stem side up. Fill the cavity between the stems with cooked meat, packing it as tightly as possible. Turn the cauliflower over, gently pull the flowerets apart and fill with as much meat as possible. Heat the remaining oil over medium heat and add the mustard seeds. As soon as the seeds pop, add the cumin and the curry leaves. Place the cauliflower in the seasoned oil, right way up, and cook, uncovered, for 2-3 minutes. Turn it over and cook the other side for 2-3 minutes. Turn the cauliflower over again and arrange any remaining meat around it. Cover the pan and turn the heat down as low as possible. Cook for 10-15 minutes or until the cauliflower is tender.

Place the cauliflower on a warmed serving dish and arrange any surplus meat around it. Garnish with the tomatoes and cilantro leaves.

KEEMA METHI
(MEAT WITH FENUGREEK)

"Methi" is the Indian word for fenugreek. It is easy to find as seeds or ground, but you may have to visit a specialist Indian shop to find the leaves.

Serves 4

INGREDIENTS
1 onion, chopped
2 tbsps ghee or oil
4 small green cardamoms
1 inch cinnamon stick
1 bay leaf
6 cloves
1 tsp fresh root ginger, peeled and grated
2-3 cloves garlic, peeled and crushed
1 pound ground beef or lamb
1 tsp chili powder
2 tsps ground coriander
2 tsps ground cumin
¼ tsp ground turmeric
⅔ cup plain yogurt
Salt
1 bunch fresh methi (fenugreek) leaves, stripped from stems and chopped *or* 1 tbsp dry kasuri methi leaves

Fry the onion in the ghee or oil until soft, then add the cardamoms, cinnamon stick, bay leaf and cloves and fry for 1 minute. Add the ginger and garlic and cook for 1 minute, then add the meat. Stir the mixture and add the chili, coriander, cumin and turmeric. Mix well and cook for 5 minutes. Beat the yogurt with the methi and add it to the pan. Cover and cook until the liquid is absorbed. Season with salt to taste before serving.

GOAN CURRY

Goa, a state of western India, formerly part of Portuguese India, is now a very popular holiday resort. This curry is typical of the food of the area – coconut is one of the principal crops.

Serves 4

INGREDIENTS
4 tbsps ghee *or* 3 tbsps oil
1 large onion, chopped
1 bay leaf
1 inch cinnamon stick
5 green cardamoms
6 cloves
3 cloves garlic, peeled and
  crushed
1 tsp fresh root ginger, peeled
  and grated
8 curry leaves
1 pound lean pork, diced
1 tbsp tamarind pulp
⅔ cup plain yogurt
¼ tsp ground turmeric
1 tsp freshly ground black
  pepper
1 tsp ground cumin
1 tsp ground coriander
½ tsp sugar
1 tbsp flaked coconut
Salt
⅔ cup water
1 tbsp freshly chopped cilantro
  leaves
2 green chilies, chopped

Heat the ghee or oil and fry the onion until golden brown. Add the bay leaf, cinnamon, cardamoms, cloves, garlic, ginger and curry leaves and fry for 1-2 minutes. Add the pork and fry for 5-7 minutes, until all the juice has evaporated. Add the tamarind pulp, yogurt, turmeric, black pepper, cumin, coriander, sugar, coconut and salt to taste. Mix well, cover and cook for 20-30 minutes. Add a little extra water if the mixture is too dry.

Add the chopped cilantro and chili, cover and cook for 20-25 minutes or until pork is tender. The dish should have a smooth gravy.

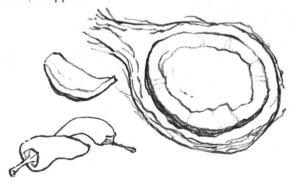

TALI KALEJI/GURDA/DIL
(MIXED FRY)

Not everyone likes the types of meat in this dish but this curry brings out their full flavor. Serve with rice or chapatis and an Indian salad or raita.

Serves 4

INGREDIENTS

½ pound pig's liver, cut into small dice

4 lambs' kidneys, halved and cored

2 hearts, cored and cut into 1-inch pieces

Salt

1 tsp chili powder

2 tsps ground coriander

¼ tsp ground turmeric

2-3 cloves garlic, peeled and crushed

1 tsp fresh root ginger, peeled and finely grated

3 tbsps ghee or oil

1 lemon

Rinse all the meats in lightly salted water and remove any fat and sinew. Drain well and toss in the chili powder, coriander, turmeric and garlic, then set aside for 5 minutes.

Melt the ghee or oil in a large pan and add the meat mixture. Cook gently for 40-45 minutes, stirring occasionally. Add salt to taste. The color will change to a rich dark brown. When the mixture is dry and the oil separates, remove from the heat and sprinkle with lemon juice. If the mixture becomes too dry during cooking, add a little water or stock.

PULSES, RICE & BREADS

Pulse vegetables are essential to classic Indian cooking, and to the everyday fare of the vast majority of Indian people. They are served as an accompaniment to meat or chicken dishes in wealthier households, but for many thousands of Indians they are the staple food, eaten daily and very often for two meals a day. For those who cannot afford to eat meat or who have adopted a vegetarian diet for religious reasons, pulses are the main source of protein and also provide a useful amount of B group vitamins.

A Variety of Flavors

My one criticism of cooking with pulse vegetables is that the resulting dishes so often taste the same, whatever pulse has been used. It is a challenge to a cook to produce tasty and interesting dishes with pulse vegetables and the Indians have a classic tradition of doing so through their imaginative and innovative use of spices. Most dhals are spiced in some way – some have a garnish of spices roasted in ghee or butter poured over them just before serving, in the same way as a Mediterranean cook might pour a little extra virgin olive oil over a dish at the last moment.

A dhal may be as spicy or mild as you like. Very bland dhals are given to young children and invalids, providing a nutritious and easily digestible meal. Others may be so highly spiced that they would dominate most curries and are served simply with plain rice or breads.

Get Organized!

Most dried pulse vegetables require soaking before use, otherwise they simply will not soften. The best way to soak is in cold water for a minimum of 8 hours or overnight. If you are really in a hurry, add boiling water and then cook the covered pulses in a large covered bowl in a microwave, for 10 minutes on full power, and then leave them for just one hour. This gives a reasonable result – but is not a classic Indian technique! Red lentils are one of the few pulses which do not require soaking and they cook very quickly, making them an invaluable store cupboard ingredient.

Rice – Basic Rules for Success

I wish to pass on a few tips for successful rice cookery. A whole meal may be marred by a dish of gelatinous grains stuck together in a lump, so it is important to perfect the art of cooking rice.

Most Indian dishes are best when cooked with basmati rice, a fine long grain of delicate flavor. It must, however, be thoroughly washed to remove all the excess starch before it is cooked, otherwise not only will it stick together, it will also boil over and make a mess of your cooker. Place the rice in a sifter and wash it under cold water until the water runs clear – this may take up to 5 minutes.

The Less Fuss the Better

Do not fiddle with rice during cooking – leave it to its own devices. Bring it to a boil in the prescribed amount of water with a pinch of salt in an open pan and then stir it once to prevent it from sticking to the base of the pan. Cover the pan tightly and cook for the recommended time, then remove the pan from the heat and leave it, covered and undisturbed, for a minimum of 10 minutes. Fork through the rice gently before serving to separate the grains and you should have a perfect result. If you are not following a recipe which gives quantities for rice and water, cook one measure of rice with two of water – the rice will absorb all the water as it cooks.

Flat Breads for Feasting

Most Indian breads are unleavened, and are therefore relatively quick to cook. The exceptions are naan and batura, a rich dough made with egg and yogurt. Many breads are cooked in a dry pan, although some are baked or fried.

Chapatis and naan are both often available in shops and are useful standbys when time is short. There can, however, be no substitute for making your own Indian breads. I think this is especially true of naan as I like to flavor it either with golden raisins, flaked almonds and spices, or a little spiced ground beef or lamb.

A meal of bread, dhal and raita or salad may not sound very exciting but when the dhal and the breads are both home-made such a meal is a veritable feast, combining delightful flavors and textures.

RAZMA (RED KIDNEY BEAN CURRY)

Red kidney beans make a colorful, tasty curry. Remember to boil them rapidly for 10 minutes at the start of their cooking period to destroy any toxins in the beans.

Serves 4

INGREDIENTS

1¼ cups red kidney beans, washed
2¼ cups water
1 tsp baking soda
4 tbsps ghee *or* 3 tbsps oil
1 onion, chopped
1 inch cinnamon stick
1 bay leaf
3 brown cardamoms
1 tsp fresh root ginger, peeled and finely grated
4 cloves garlic, peeled and crushed
1 tsp chili powder
1 tsp ground coriander
1 tsp garam masala
¼ tsp turmeric
7-ounce can chopped tomatoes
Salt to taste
2 green chilies, halved
1 tbsp freshly chopped cilantro leaves

Soak the kidney beans in the water with baking soda overnight. Drain the beans, rinse and boil in fresh water for 1 hour or until the beans are cooked. Cool and strain the beans, retaining the cooking liquid.

Heat the ghee or oil and fry the onion for 2-3 minutes. Add the cinnamon, bay leaf, cardamoms, ginger and garlic. Cook for 1 minute, then add the chili powder, ground coriander, garam masala and turmeric. Stir the spices well. Add the tomatoes and salt, then the kidney beans, and fry the mixture for 2-3 minutes. Add ¾-1 cup of the bean cooking liquor, the green chili and chopped cilantro. Simmer for 15-20 minutes. Add more bean liquor if the sauce is too thick. Transfer the Razma to a warmed dish and serve.

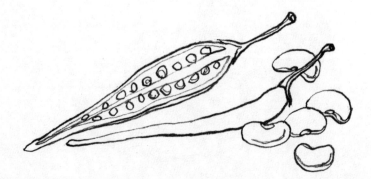

ALOO CHOLE

Use canned garbanzo beans to make this dish if you are in a hurry – they will not provide the same texture as freshly cooked ones but are a good stand-by in the store cupboard.

Serves 4-6

INGREDIENTS
1¼ cups garbanzo beans, sorted through
4 cups water
½-inch piece of fresh root ginger, peeled and grated
1 large potato, peeled and cut into 1½-inch dice
1 tsp ground cumin
½ tsp ground turmeric
¼-½ tsp chili powder (optional)
1-2 fresh green chilies, slit lengthwise into halves, de-seeded for a mild flavor
2 tbsps ghee or sweet butter
1 large onion, finely chopped
1¼ tsps salt
½ tsp garam masala
1 tbsp lemon juice
1 tbsp freshly chopped fresh mint *or* 1 tsp dried mint

Soak the garbanzo beans overnight in plenty of cold water. Rinse several times and drain well. Place the beans, water and ginger in a large pan over high heat. Bring to a boil, cover the pan and simmer for 1¼-1½ hours or until the beans are tender. Add the potato, cumin, turmeric, chili powder and green chilies. (If you are using dried mint, add it now.) Return to a boil, cover the pan and simmer for a further 15-20 minutes, until the potatoes are tender.

Melt the ghee over medium heat and fry the onion until it is lightly browned. Stir it into the garbanzo beans with the salt and garam masala. Remove the pan from the heat and stir in the lemon juice and fresh mint (if used). Serve immediately.

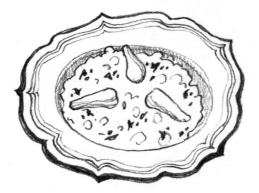

LOBIA CURRY (BLACK EYED PEA CURRY)

A curry with a thick tomato sauce, ideal to serve with brown rice and salad.

Serves 4

INGREDIENTS

1¼ cups lobia (black eyed peas), washed and soaked overnight in water
2¼ cups water
1 onion, chopped
4 tbsps ghee *or* 3 tbsps oil
1 bay leaf
1 inch cinnamon stick
1 tsp fresh root ginger, peeled and grated
2-3 cloves garlic, peeled and crushed
¼ tsp ground turmeric
1 tsp ground coriander
1 tsp chili powder
4-5 canned tomatoes, crushed *or* 4 fresh tomatoes, chopped
Salt
2 green chilies, halved and chopped
2 tbsp freshly chopped cilantro leaves

Boil the soaked peas in the water for 20 minutes, then let them cool. Fry the onion in the ghee or oil for 3-4 minutes. Add the bay leaf, cinnamon, ginger and garlic. Fry for 2 minutes, then add the turmeric, ground coriander and chili powder, and stir well. Add the beans, tomatoes, salt, chopped chili and cilantro. Cover and simmer for 10-15 minutes.

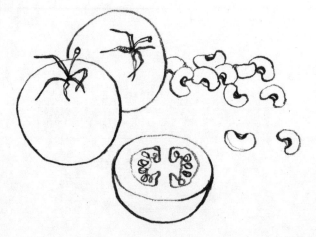

CHANA MASALA

This is a medium hot curry of garbanzo beans – use canned garbanzo beans if time is short. You will need two 12-ounce cans, drained.

Serves 4

INGREDIENTS

1 large onion, chopped
4 cloves garlic, peeled and crushed
1-inch piece fresh root ginger, peeled and finely chopped
3 tbsps ghee
1 tbsp ground coriander
2 tsps cumin seeds
¼ tsp cayenne pepper
1 tsp turmeric
2 tsps ground cumin
1 tbsp amchur (dried mango powder) *or* 1 tbsp lemon juice
2 tsps paprika pepper
14-ounce can tomatoes
5 cups cooked garbanzo beans (2 cups uncooked)
1 tsp garam masala
½ tsp salt
1 fresh green chili, finely chopped

Cook the onion, garlic and ginger in the ghee until soft. Add all the spices and fry over low heat for 1-2 minutes, stirring all the time. Add the tomatoes, roughly chopped, together with their juice, then add the cooked garbanzo beans. Cook for 30 minutes over medium heat.

Add the garam masala, salt and chopped chili. Stir well and serve hot.

SAAGWALLA DHAL

This dhal is very green in color and not very attractive to the eye, but the flavor is delicious. Serve topped with yogurt for a more attractive presentation.

Serves 6-8

INGREDIENTS

¾ cup skinless split moong dhal or yellow split peas

2 tbsps ghee or sweet butter

1 large onion, finely sliced

1 fresh green chili, sliced lengthwise; de-seeded for a mild flavor

2 cinnamon sticks, 2 inches long, broken up into 2-3 pieces

½ tsp ground turmeric

½ tsp garam masala

¼ tsp chili powder

1 tsp salt

1 tsp ground cumin

2 ripe tomatoes, skinned and chopped

2¼ cups warm water

2 tbsps cooking oil

½ tsp black mustard seeds

2-3 cloves garlic, peeled and finely chopped

1-2 dried red chilies, roughly chopped

¼ pound frozen leaf spinach, defrosted and finely chopped *or* ⅔ pound fresh spinach, hard stalks removed and finely chopped

Wash and soak the dhal for 1½-2 hours. Drain well. Melt the ghee or butter over medium heat in a non-stick or cast iron pan and fry the onion, green chili and cinnamon until the onion is lightly browned. Add the turmeric and garam masala. Stir and mix well, then add the dhal, chili powder and salt. Stir-fry for 8-10 minutes over low heat. Add the cumin and tomatoes, and cook for 3-4 minutes, then add the water. Bring to a boil, cover and simmer for 30-35 minutes, stirring occasionally.

Meanwhile, heat the oil over medium heat and fry the mustard seeds until they pop. Add the garlic and allow it to turn slightly brown, then add the dried red chilies and the spinach. Mix thoroughly. Cover the pan and simmer for 5 minutes. Add the spinach to the dhal. Cover and cook over low heat for 10 minutes, stirring occasionally. Serve with dry curries, topped with yogurt if liked.

SAMBHAR (DHAL AND VEGETABLE)

This is an unusual dhal, suitable for serving as a main course as it contains plenty of fresh vegetables which give it a colorful and attractive appearance.

Serves 4

INGREDIENTS
Whole Spices
1 tsp coriander seeds
1 tsp cumin seeds
2 dry red chilies (whole)
2 tsp channa dhal
¼ tsp fenugreek seeds (methi)

1 cup toor dhal
2¼ cups water
1 carrot, peeled and sliced
1 potato, peeled and diced
6-8 okra (bhindi), topped and
   tailed and cut into 1-inch
   pieces
1 small zucchini, sliced
1 small eggplant, halved and
   sliced
6 curry leaves
2 tbsps tamarind pulp
1 green chili, cut in half
Salt to taste
1 sprig fresh green cilantro leaves
1 tbsp oil
½ tsp mustard seeds
¼ tsp asafoetida (hing)

Roast the spices until lightly browned in a dry skillet over low heat. Let cool, then grind in a pestle and mortar or a coffee grinder.

Wash the dhal in 4-5 changes of water, until the water is clear. Drain. Add 1¼ cups of water, cover and simmer gently for 6-10 minutes. Remove any froth that forms with a spoon. When the dhal is soft, beat it with a potato masher or whisk until smooth.

In a separate pan, boil the carrots, potatoes, okra, zucchini and eggplant with the ground roasted spices and the remaining water for 4-5 minutes. Mix the dhal and vegetables with any remaining liquid. Add the curry leaves, tamarind pulp, salt, chopped chili and fresh cilantro. Simmer for 10-15 minutes, then turn into a warmed serving dish. Heat the oil and fry the mustard seeds and asafoetida for a half minute, then pour over the sambhar. Serve with boiled rice.

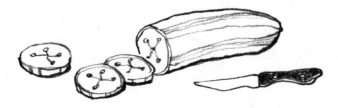

KHARI URID DHAL
(DRY URID DHAL)

*This is a dry dhal that may be served with paratha or any
Indian bread. Black beans are generally referred to as urid
dhal – without their husks or skins they are white.*

Serves 4

INGREDIENTS
1¼ cups white urid dhal,
   dehusked and washed in 3-4
   changes of water
Salt to taste
1 cup water

For Garnish
1 onion, sliced
4 tbsps sweet butter
1 green chili, chopped
1 inch fresh root ginger, peeled
   and sliced
1 tbsp freshly chopped cilantro
   leaves

Cook the urid dhal in the water,
with salt to taste, over low heat
until the water has evaporated.
Fry the onion in the butter in a
separate pan until golden brown.
Add the chopped chili and
ginger and fry for 2-3 minutes.
Pour the onion mixture over the
dhal and garnish with the
chopped cilantro.

TARKA DHAL
(SPICED LENTILS)

At least one type of dhal is always served during an Indian meal. Dhals are of vital importance in the vegetarian diet, providing protein. I find that they are popular with everyone as they reduce the overall heat of the meal.

Serves 4

INGREDIENTS

¾ cup masoor dhal (red split lentils)
3 cups water
1 tsp ground turmeric
1 tsp ground cumin
1 tsp salt
2 tbsps ghee or sweet butter
1 onion, finely chopped
2 cloves garlic, peeled and finely chopped
2 dried red chilies, roughly chopped

Place the dhal, water, turmeric, cumin and salt in a pan and bring to a boil. Lower the heat to medium and cook uncovered for 8-10 minutes, stirring frequently. Cover the pan and simmer for a further 30 minutes, stirring occasionally. Remove the dhal from the heat, let cool slightly and then press through a sifter.

Melt the ghee or butter over medium heat. Fry the onion, garlic and red chilies until the onion is well browned. Stir half the fried onion into the dhal and turn it into a warmed serving dish. Arrange the remaining fried onion on top.

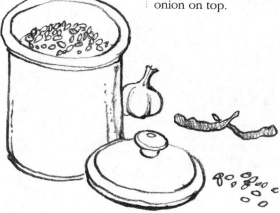

MASOOR DHAL (RED LENTIL)

Red lentils are widely available and are an excellent ingredient to keep in the store cupboard: they cook quickly and are high in protein.

Serves 4

INGREDIENTS
1 cup red lentils
2¼ cups water
1 tsp chili powder
2 tsps ground coriander
¼ tsp turmeric powder
¼ tsp salt
1 tbsp freshly chopped cilantro leaves
4 fresh tomatoes, chopped *or* 5 canned tomatoes, crushed
1 onion, chopped
4 tbsps butter
1 green chili, halved and chopped

Wash the lentils in 4-5 changes of water, until the water runs clear. Drain. Add the water and cover. Simmer gently, without stirring, for 10-15 minutes until the lentils are thoroughly cooked.

Blend the lentils with a potato masher or beat them with an egg beater. Add the chili powder, ground coriander, turmeric, salt, cilantro leaves and tomatoes, then cover and simmer for 6-8 minutes. Remove the pan from the heat. Fry the onion in the butter until brown, then pour the onion and butter over the dhal. Garnish with the chopped chili.

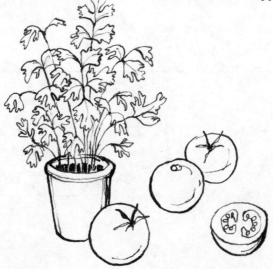

SPICY CHANNA DHAL

Channa Dhal is one of the best known side-dishes – it may also be made with yellow split peas. I like to serve it with kebabs or any chicken dish.

Serves 4-6

INGREDIENTS

1 cup channa dhal or yellow split peas
3 tbsps ghee or sweet butter
1 large onion, finely sliced
2 cinnamon sticks, 2 inches long, broken up into 2-3 pieces
6 green cardamoms, the top of each pod split open
2-4 dried red chilies, roughly chopped
½ tsp ground turmeric
¼-½ tsp chili powder
1¼ tsps salt
2¼ cups warm water
2 bay leaves, crushed
½ cup flaked coconut
2 ripe tomatoes, skinned and chopped
2 tbsps freshly chopped cilantro leaves (optional)

Clean and wash the channa dahl or the yellow split peas and soak them for at least 2 hours. Drain well. Melt the ghee or butter over medium heat and fry the onion, cinnamon, cardamoms and red chilies until the onion is lightly browned. Add the dhal, turmeric, chili powder and salt. Stir-fry for 2-3 minutes. Lower the heat and fry the dhal for a further 3-4 minutes, stirring frequently. Add the water, bay leaves, coconut and tomatoes. Bring to a boil, cover the pan and simmer for 35-40 minutes. Stir in the cilantro leaves (if using) and season to taste with extra salt if required.

SABUT MASOOR
(WHOLE LENTIL)

This dhal should be made with whole lentils, either brown or green. I prefer to soak them overnight to give a softer, smoother consistency. Add a little extra water if necessary to give a moist consistency.

Serves 4

INGREDIENTS

4 tbsps butter
1 onion, chopped
1 bay leaf
1 inch cinnamon stick
1 tsp fresh root ginger, peeled and finely grated
2 cloves garlic, peeled and crushed
1 cup dhal, washed in 3-4 changes of water
2 cups water
1 tsp ground coriander
½ tsp chili powder
¼ tsp turmeric powder
3 fresh tomatoes, chopped *or* 3 canned tomatoes, chopped
1 green chili, chopped
1 tbsp freshly chopped cilantro leaves
Salt to taste

Heat the butter and fry the onion until golden brown. Add the bay leaf, cinnamon stick, ginger and garlic and fry for 1 minute. Add the drained dhal and water. Cover, bring to a boil and simmer gently for 12-15 minutes. The dhal should be well cooked. Beat it until smooth, then add the ground coriander, chili and turmeric powder. Stir in the tomatoes, green chili and fresh cilantro. Season with salt and mix well. Cover and cook gently for 7-10 minutes.

Season the dhal with extra salt if necessary. Serve with rice or chapatis and a vegetable curry.

GREEN LENTILS WITH FRESH GINGER AND SPICES

This spicy lentil dish is ideal for vegetarians, served with brown rice and a cucumber or vegetable raita.

Serves 4

INGREDIENTS
¾ cup green lentils
Water or stock to cover
2 tbsps ghee or sweet butter
1 onion, finely chopped
1-inch piece fresh root ginger, peeled and grated or finely chopped
1 tsp garam masala
1 tsp cumin seeds
1 tsp coriander seeds, crushed
1 tsp green cardamom pods, seeds removed and crushed
1 carrot, peeled and diced
14-ounce can tomatoes
½ cup finely chopped mushrooms
Salt
1 tbsp cider vinegar
Freshly ground black pepper
Lemon slices
Freshly chopped parsley or cilantro leaves to garnish

Sort through the lentils and wash them thoroughly. Place the lentils in a large, heavy based pan, cover with water or stock and bring to a boil. Turn off the heat, cover and leave the lentils until they begin to swell.

Meanwhile, heat the ghee or butter in a separate pan. Gently fry the onion, ginger and spices until they are well combined and give off a tempting aroma. Add the mixture to the lentils and bring to a boil. Start to add the remaining vegetables, allowing several minutes between each addition; begin with the carrot, then add the tomatoes and lastly the chopped mushrooms. Stir frequently to prevent sticking and check on the liquid regularly, adding more water or stock as necessary.

Just before the end of the cooking time – approximately 25 minutes – add the salt, cider vinegar and pepper. Cook for a few more minutes and serve hot, garnished with slices of lemon and freshly chopped parsley or cilantro.

ARHAR TOOR DHAL (YELLOW LENTIL)

This yellow lentil dhal has a thick, smooth consistency. It is best served with rice and a chunky vegetable curry, and a selection of relishes.

Serves 4

INGREDIENTS
1 cup toor dhal
2¼ cups water
¼ tsp turmeric powder
1 tsp ground coriander
¼ tsp salt
6 curry leaves
1 green chili, split in half
1 tbsp fresh or flaked coconut
1 tbsp freshly chopped cilantro leaves
4 tbsps butter
1 tsp mustard seeds

Wash the toor dhal in 4-5 changes of water, then drain. Add the water, turmeric, salt and coriander. Cover and simmer gently for 10-15 minutes, until the dhal is well cooked and soft. Beat vigorously until smooth, then add the curry leaves, coconut, chili and cilantro leaves. Cover and cook for a further 8-10 minutes.

Heat the butter and fry the mustard seeds for 30 seconds, then pour them over the dhal. Serve with rice or rotis.

BESAN LADOO

Besan is ground garbanzo beans. It is generally used as a thickener or a batter ingredient, but in this recipe it is made into a sweetmeat.

Makes 28-30

INGREDIENTS
1 cup ghee or sweet butter
2½ cups besan, sifted to remove the husks
1 cup sugar
1½ tsps ground cardamom seeds
¼ cup broken nut meats

Melt the ghee or butter in a pan over medium heat and add the besan. Lower the heat and fry the besan for 12-15 minutes, stirring continuously. Add the rest of the ingredients, mix thoroughly, then remove the pan from the heat. Let the mixture cool completely, then form into small walnut-size balls.

Store in an airtight container. The besan ladoo will remain fresh for 4-5 weeks.

PLAIN FRIED RICE

I often think that boiled rice is too plain to serve with curry, yet it is quick and simple to prepare. This recipe for Plain Fried Rice produces lightly spiced rice, requiring the minimum of preparation, which is suitable to serve with almost any curry.

Serves 4-6

INGREDIENTS
1½ cups basmati or other long-grain rice, washed and soaked in cold water for ½-1 hour
2 tbsps ghee *or* 3 tbsps cooking oil
1 tsp fennel seeds
1 tsp salt
2¼ cups water for basmati rice *or* 2½ cups for other long-grain rice

Drain the rice and set aside. Heat the oil or ghee over medium heat and fry the fennel seeds until they are brown. Add the rice and salt. Stir and cook for 4-5 minutes, lowering the heat for the last 2-3 minutes of cooking. Add the water to the pan and bring to a boil. Cover and simmer for 12 minutes for basmati rice and 15-18 minutes for long-grain rice without lifting the lid. Leave undisturbed, off the heat, for 10 minutes before serving.

PILAF RICE

Pilaf rice can be a plain dish or have meat, chicken or fish added to it. It is always fragrant and full of flavor.

Serves 4-6

INGREDIENTS
1½ cups basmati rice
4 tbsps ghee or sweet butter
1 large onion, finely sliced
2-4 cloves garlic, peeled and finely chopped
8 whole cloves
8 green cardamoms, the top of each pod split open
2 cinnamon sticks, 2 inches long, broken up
8 whole peppercorns
1 tsp ground turmeric
2½ cups water
1¼ tsps salt
1 tbsp butter
¼ cup golden raisins
1 cup flaked almonds

Wash the rice and soak in cold water for 30 minutes. Drain well. Melt the ghee or butter in a heavy based pan over medium heat and fry the onion until it is soft but not brown. Add the garlic, cloves, cardamoms, cinnamon sticks and peppercorns. Stir-fry until the onion is golden brown, then add the rice and turmeric, and cook for 1-2 minutes. Lower the heat and cook the rice for a further 2-3 minutes. Add the water and the salt, bring to a boil, and cover and simmer for 15 minutes without lifting the lid.

Remove the pan from the heat and leave undisturbed for a further 10-12 minutes. Melt the butter over gentle heat and fry the golden raisins until they change color and swell. Transfer the golden raisins to a plate and, in the same fat, fry the almonds until they are lightly browned. Remove to a separate plate. Pile the pilaf rice into a warmed serving dish and, using a fork, gently mix in the fried golden raisins and almonds.

FRIED BROWN RICE

You might think this recipe would use brown rice with husks, but no! The rice is almost caramelized in sugar and is quite delicious. This is the classic accompaniment to dhansak curries, but it can be served with any dish.

Serves 4-6

INGREDIENTS
1½ cups basmati or other long-grain rice
4 tbsps cooking oil
4 tsps sugar
1 tsp cumin seeds
2 cinnamon sticks, 2 inches long, broken up
6 whole cloves
6 black peppercorns
2 bay leaves, crushed
2½ cups water
1 tsp salt

Wash the rice and soak in cold water for 30 minutes. Drain well. Heat the oil over medium heat in a heavy based pan and add the sugar. The sugar will gradually begin to change color to dark brown. As soon as it does, add the cumin seeds, cinnamon, cloves, black peppercorns and bay leaves. Fry for 30 seconds. Add the rice and cook for about 5 minutes, stirring frequently and lowering the heat for the last minute or two. Add the water and salt. Bring to a boil, cover and simmer without lifting the lid. Cook for 12-15 minutes for basmati rice, or 15-18 minutes for long-grain rice. Remove the pan from the heat and leave it undisturbed for a further 10-15 minutes before serving.

CARDAMOM RICE

Cardamoms have a most distinctive flavor – I remember munching them with an Indian friend to clear the taste buds after a very heavy meal. This rice is more subtly flavored than many pilafs, making it ideal for serving with even the mildest of curries.

Serves 4-6

INGREDIENTS

1½ cups basmati or other long-grain rice
4 tbsps ghee or sweet butter
6 green cardamoms, the top of each pod split open
1 tsp black cumin seeds or caraway seeds
1 tsp salt
2¼ cups water for basmati rice *or* 2½ cups for other long-grain rice

Wash the rice, soak in cold water for ½-1 hour and drain thoroughly. Melt the ghee or butter in a large pan over low heat and fry the cardamoms and cumin or caraway seeds for 1 minute. Add the rice. Stir and cook over medium heat for 2-3 minutes, then lower the heat and cook for a further 2-3 minutes. Add the salt and water and mix well. Bring to a boil, cover the pan and simmer for 12 minutes for basmati rice and 15-18 minutes for long-grain rice without lifting the lid. Remove from the heat and leave the pan undisturbed for 6-8 minutes.

BASMATI RICE WITH VEGETABLES

*Basmati is sometimes called "the Prince of rices" – it
certainly produces the best and most tasty results but only if
washed for some minutes under running water before being
cooked. Keep washing until the water runs clear and all the
starch has been removed from the rice.*

Serves 4

INGREDIENTS
1 red pepper, de-seeded
1 green pepper, de-seeded
1 zucchini
1 carrot
2 shallots
½ vanilla pod
2 pinches of cinnamon
1 pinch of powdered saffron
½ tsp turmeric
½ tsp curry powder
3 cardamom seeds
3 tbsps oil
1¾ cups basmati rice
1 bouquet garni
2½ cups water
Salt and freshly ground black
  pepper
Fresh cilantro leaves

Cut the peppers into even-size strips. Cut the zucchini into chunks, then slices and finally matchsticks. Cut the carrot into slightly smaller matchsticks. Cut the shallots in half and chop finely. Slit open the vanilla pod and run the tip of a knife blade down the inside to extract the seeds. Mix the seeds with the cinnamon, saffron, turmeric, curry powder and cardamom.

Heat the oil in a baking dish and fry the vegetables for 5 minutes, stirring frequently. When cooked through, add the rice and bouquet garni. Continue frying until the rice becomes transparent. Add the spices and some salt and pepper to the water, then add to the rice and do not stir again. Cover and cook in a 425°F oven for 25 minutes. When cooked, fluff up the rice with a fork and serve garnished with fresh cilantro.

SRI LANKAN RICE

This is a colorful rice dish, suitable for serving hot with curries or cold as a salad

Serves 4

INGREDIENTS

3 tbsps sunflower oil
1 onion, finely chopped
2 cloves garlic, peeled and crushed
1 tsp ground cumin
1 tsp ground coriander
1 tsp paprika pepper
2 tsps turmeric
¼ tsp chili powder *or* cayenne pepper
¾ cup basmati rice, washed and drained
¾ cup milk
1 tsp salt
Freshly ground black pepper to taste
½ pound snow peas, topped, tailed and cut in half
¼ pound mushrooms, washed and sliced
1¼ cups sweetcorn
⅓ cup golden raisins, washed and soaked

Heat the oil in a large non-stick pan and gently fry the onion and garlic for 4-5 minutes. Add the cumin, coriander, paprika, turmeric and chili. Lower the heat and fry for a further 3-4 minutes – do not allow the mixture to burn. Add the washed rice, mix well and cook with the onion and spices for about 2 minutes. Add the milk, salt and pepper and stir gently. Bring to a boil. Cover and simmer until all the liquid is absorbed and the rice is cooked – approximately 15-20 minutes.

Whilst the rice is cooking, steam the snow peas, mushrooms, sweetcorn and golden raisins for 6-8 minutes. Fold the vegetables into the rice after it has stood undisturbed for 10 minutes. Serve hot.

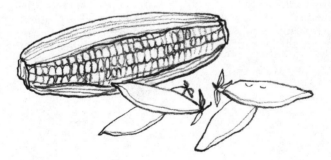

MIXED VEGETABLE PILAF

A colorful, well flavored pilaf that is quick to prepare. I serve this with Tandoori Chicken or fish. Soak the rice while you prepare the vegetables.

Serves 6

INGREDIENTS
4 tbsps ghee or sweet butter
1 large onion, finely sliced
3-4 cloves garlic, peeled and
 finely chopped

Spices
1 tsp black cumin seeds or
 caraway seeds
1 tsp coriander seeds
6 black peppercorns
1 bay leaf
2 dried red chilies
1 cinnamon stick, 2 inches long,
 broken up
6 green cardamoms

½ tsp ground turmeric
½ pound cauliflower flowerets,
 cut into ½-inch pieces
1 small green pepper, de-seeded
 and cut into 1-inch strips
⅔ cup thinly sliced carrots
1½ cups basmati rice, washed
 and soaked in cold water for
 30 minutes and drained
½ cup frozen garden peas or
 fresh peas boiled until nearly
 tender
½ cup frozen sweetcorn
1½ tsps salt
2½ cups water

Melt the ghee or butter in a large pan over medium heat and fry the onions and garlic until golden brown. Grind the seven spices in a pestle and mortar and add with the turmeric. Fry for 2 minutes over low heat, stirring frequently. Add the cauliflower, green pepper and carrots; stir and cook for 2-3 minutes. Stir in the rice and cook for a further 2-3 minutes, stirring constantly. Finally, add the peas, sweetcorn and salt, and stir well. Add the water, bring to a boil, cover the pan and simmer for about 12-15 minutes until the rice has absorbed all the water. Allow about 18 minutes for other types of long-grain rice. Do not lift the lid or stir the rice during cooking.

Remove the pan from the heat, uncover, and allow the steam to escape for 2 minutes. Do not stir the rice immediately after cooking. Cover the pan and leave it undisturbed for 10 minutes before serving.

MATTAR PILAF

This is a simple pilaf rice with peas giving extra color and flavor – frozen peas are ideal. The rice is colored yellow with turmeric, a cheap alternative for saffron.

Serves 4-6

INGREDIENTS

1½ cups basmati rice
6 tbsps ghee or sweet butter
2 tsps fennel seeds
2-3 dried red chilies
6 whole cloves
2 cinnamon sticks, each 2 inches long, broken up
6 green cardamoms, the top of each pod split open
2 bay leaves, crushed
1 large onion, finely sliced
1½ cups frozen garden peas
1 tsp ground turmeric
1¼ tsps salt, or to taste
2½ cups water

Wash the rice and soak it in cold water for a half hour. Drain thoroughly. Melt the ghee or butter over medium heat and fry the fennel seeds until they are brown. Add the chilies, cloves, cinnamon, cardamom and bay leaves. Stir once and add the onion, then fry until the onion is lightly browned, stirring frequently. Add the rice, peas, turmeric and salt. Stir-fry for 4-5 minutes, until the rice is fairly dry, lowering the heat for the last 1-2 minutes. Add the water and bring to a boil. Cover the pan and simmer for 12-15 minutes without lifting the lid. Remove the pan from the heat and leave it undisturbed for a further 10-15 minutes. Fork through the rice and serve.

MUSHROOM PILAF

Mushrooms and rice blend well to make a tasty pilaf. Serve with a plain vegetable curry or a meat curry of your choice.

Serves 4-6

INGREDIENTS
1½ cups basmati rice
4 tbsps ghee or sweet butter
1 tsp caraway seeds
1 large onion, finely sliced
2 cinnamon sticks, each 2 inches long, broken up
½ pound button mushrooms, thickly sliced
½ tsp ground turmeric
1¼ tsps salt
2¼ cups water
6 green cardamoms, the top of each pod split open
6 whole cloves
2 bay leaves, crushed

Wash and soak the rice in cold water for 30 minutes. Drain and set aside. Melt the ghee or butter over medium heat and fry the caraway seeds for 30 seconds. Add the onion and cinnnamon sticks, and cook until the onion is golden brown. Add the rice and fry, stirring constantly, for 3-4 minutes. Add the mushrooms, turmeric and salt. Stir and cook for a further 2-3 minutes over low heat.

Add the water, cardamoms, cloves and bay leaves to the pan. Bring to a boil, cover and simmer for 12-15 minutes. Do not lift the lid or stir the rice during cooking. Remove the pan from the heat, uncover and let the steam escape for 1-2 minutes. Cover the pan and leave for 10-15 minutes before serving.

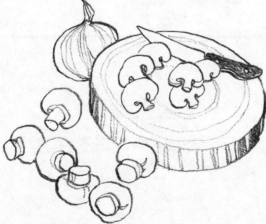

CARROT PILAF

The younger the carrots, the sweeter the flavor that they will impart to this colorful pilaf. Serve with any meat, fish or chicken curry.

Serves 4-6

INGREDIENTS

1½ cups basmati rice, washed and soaked in cold water for ½ hour
2¼ cups water
1 tsp salt
3 tbsps ghee or sweet butter
1 tsp cumin or caraway seeds
1 onion, finely sliced
2 cinnamon sticks, each 2 inches long, broken up
4 green cardamoms, the top of each pod split open
1 tsp garam masala or ground mixed spice
1 cup coarsely grated carrots
1 cup frozen peas
½ tsp salt

Drain the rice thoroughly and place it in a pan with the water. Bring to a boil, then stir in the salt and 1 tsp of ghee or butter. Boil the rice steadily for 1 minute, then cover the pan and simmer for 12-15 minutes. Do not lift the lid during this time. Remove the pan from the heat and keep it covered for a further 10 minutes.

Meanwhile, prepare the rest of the ingredients. Melt the remaining ghee or butter over medium heat and fry the cumin or caraway seeds until they crackle. Add the onion, cinnamon and cardamom. Fry until the onion is lightly browned, stirring frequently. Add the garam masala or ground mixed spice, stir-fry for 30 seconds. Add the carrots, peas and salt, stir and cook for 1-2 minutes. Add the cooked rice, stir and mix gently using a metal spoon or a fork – a wooden spoon or spatula will squash the grains. Remove the pan from the heat and serve.

NAAN

I have watched naan breads being cooked, pressed against the sides of a tandoor on special sticks. They will cook well at home in a very hot oven.

Makes 8 naan

INGREDIENTS
4 cups all-purpose flour
1 tsp salt
1 tsp kalonji (onion seeds)
  (optional)
1 tsp sugar
1½ sachets dry active yeast
6 tbsps milk
⅔ cup plain yogurt
1 medium-size egg, beaten
4 tbsps ghee or butter
2 tbsps sesame seeds or white
  poppy seeds

Place the flour, salt, kalonji (if used), sugar and yeast in a large bowl and mix well. Heat the milk until it is lukewarm. Reserve 1 tbsp of yogurt and add the rest to the milk and blend thoroughly. Beat the egg and set to one side. Melt the butter or ghee.

Add the milk and yogurt mixture, the egg and ghee or butter to the flour, and knead with your hands or in a food processor or mixer until a soft and springy dough is formed. Place the dough in a large plastic bag. Loosely seal the bag, so that the dough has enough room for expansion.

Leave in a warm place for 30-60 minutes, until doubled in size. Divide the dough into 8 balls, cover them and set aside for 10-15 minutes.

Switch on the oven and put an ungreased baking sheet into it for about 10 minutes. Remove the baking sheet from the oven and line it with waxed paper or baking parchment. Take one of the balls and stretch it gently with both hands to make a teardrop shape. Lay this on the baking sheet and press it gently to stretch it until about 6-7 inches in length, maintaining the teardrop shape at all times. Make 2-3 similar shapes for one batch and brush with the reserved yogurt, then sprinkle with the sesame or poppy seeds. Bake on the top shelf of a 450°F oven for 10-12 minutes, or until puffed and browned. Keep the naan warm in a clean dishcloth or a foil package whilst cooking the remaining breads.

PARATHAS

Indian breads are fun to make and very quick to cook as they are generally fried or grilled. We often make our own for a weekend curry.

Makes 4 parathas

INGREDIENTS
3 cups whole wheat flour or chapati flour (atta) plus 1 tbsp extra flour for dusting
½ tsp salt
⅔ cup ghee or sweet butter
½-⅔ cup warm water

Sift the flour and salt together in a bowl. Rub ¼ cup of the fat into the flour until thoroughly mixed. Gradually pour in the water, mixing and kneading the mixture to a soft, pliable dough. Divide the dough into 4 equal pieces and flatten them by pressing gently with the palms of your hands.

Dust each flattened piece of dough with the flour and roll out to a circle 8 inches in diameter. Spread a knob of the remaining fat over each circle of dough. Roll the parathas up into tubes about 1 inch in diameter and 8 inches long. Gently stretch the dough lengthwise and then curl each end inwards in an anti-clockwise direction to resemble a back-to-front letter "S." Fold the upper half onto the lower and flatten. Lightly dust all over with flour and roll out the paratha again until the dough is about 8 inches in diameter and very thin.

Melt the remaining fat and keep to one side. Heat a skillet (preferably a cast iron one) over medium heat and place a paratha in it. Turn it over after 30 seconds. Spread 1 tablespoon of the melted fat over the paratha. Flip it over again, lower the heat, and spread 1 tablespoon of the melted fat on the second side of the bread. Press the paratha into the pan with a spatula, keeping the dough in contact with the pan. Cook for 1 minute, then turn and cook the second side in the same way. Continue cooking for a few minutes, until the paratha is light brown all over. Wrap in a clean cloth to keep warm while cooking the remaining parathas.

ROTIS

These are unleavened whole wheat breads. I have made them successfully using a mixture of flours.

Makes 8 rotis

INGREDIENTS
½ tsp salt
¼ cup butter or ghee
3 cups atta/chapati flour *or* 1½ cups each of whole wheat and all-purpose flour
¾-1¼ cups warm water (the quantity depends on the texture of the flour)
2 tbsps ghee or sweet butter for frying

Rub the salt and fat into the flour until you reach a rough breadcrumb consistency. Gradually add the water and mix to a soft, pliable dough. Knead lightly, then divide the dough into 8. Roll into balls between the palms of your hands, then flatten the balls into round cakes and dust them very lightly with a little all-purpose flour. Roll each into a circle about 6 inches in diameter. Cover the rest of the dough with a damp cloth while you are working on each roti.

Heat a heavy based skillet over medium heat; it is important to use a heavy based pan as the rotis need even distribution of heat to cook properly. When the pan is hot, place a roti in it and flip it over after about 30 seconds. Spread 1 tsp of ghee or butter over it and turn the roti over. Repeat the process for the other side. Brown both sides evenly and remove from the heat. Line a piece of foil with paper towels and put the cooked rotis on one end. Cover with the other end and seal the edges to make a foil package. This will keep the rotis warm for 30-40 minutes.

CHAPATIS

These are the best known of all the Indian unleavened breads. They are not too filling, so people may eat two or three, especially if you are not serving rice.

Makes 14 chapatis

3 cups fine whole wheat flour or atta/chapati flour
½ tsp salt
3 tbsps butter or ghee
¾-1¼ cups warm water (the quantity depends on the texture of the flour)
1 tbsp extra flour in a shallow bowl or plate.

Place the flour and salt in a large bowl and rub in the fat. Gradually add the water and keep mixing and kneading until a soft and pliable dough is formed. Cover the dough with a damp cloth and leave in a warm place for 30-60 minutes.

Divide the dough into 14 walnut-size pieces. Roll each one into a ball, then flatten the ball to make a round cake. Dip each cake into the dry flour and roll the chapati into a circle about 6 inches in diameter. An iron griddle is normally used for cooking chapatis, but if you do not have one, then use a heavy based skillet – the chapatis need even distribution of heat during cooking. Overheating the pan will cause them to stick and burn.

Heat the griddle or skillet over medium heat and place a chapati in it. Cook for 30 seconds, then turn the chapati over. Cook until brown spots appear on both sides, turning the chapati over frequently. To keep the chapatis warm, line a piece of foil with paper towels and place the chapatis on one end. Cover with the other end and seal the edges, making a foil package. Repeat the cooking method until all the chapatis are cooked. Serve hot or warm.

BATURA

*This unusual bread is made with yogurt, which gives it a
soft, rich texture. The breads are deep-fried after shaping.*

Serves 6

INGREDIENTS
3 cups all-purpose flour
1 tsp salt
2 tsps dry active yeast
1 egg, beaten
⅔ cup plain yogurt
2-3 tbsps warm water
Oil for deep-frying

Place the flour, salt and yeast in a
bowl and mix well. Add the egg,
yogurt and water and mix until a
soft, pliable dough is formed.
Alternatively, put all the
ingredients in the bowl of a food
processor which has a dough
hook, and mix until the dough is
formed. Knead the dough lightly
and place it in a large plastic bag.
Seal the bag loosely, leaving
room for the dough to expand.

Leave the dough to rise in a
warm place for 3-4 hours, or
until doubled in size.

Remove the dough from the bag
and divide it into 6 pieces. Shape
into balls, then flatten into round
cakes. Dust lightly with a little
flour and roll out into circles
about 6 inches in diameter.

Heat the oil to 350°F; take care
not to overheat it. Place a batura
in the hot oil and fry it for 1
minute; turn it over and fry the
other side for a further minute or
until it is a rich creamy color.
Drain on paper towels. Roll and
fry all the baturas in the same
way. It is easier to roll and fry
one batura at a time than to roll
them all out at once.

LOOCHIS

Loochis are deep-fried puffs of Indian bread, similar to puris. They are made with ordinary all-purpose flour and I find them ideal to serve with appetizers.

Makes 14-15 loochis

INGREDIENTS

2½ cups all-purpose flour plus 1 tbsp extra flour for dusting
½ tsp salt
¼ tsp sugar
1 tsp kalonji (onion seeds) (optional)
1 tbsp butter, margarine or ghee
⅔-¾ cup warm water (this will depend on the texture of the flour)
Oil for deep-frying

In a large bowl, mix together the flour, salt, sugar and kalonji (if used). Rub in the fat and gradually add the water. Either knead with your hands or in a food processor until a stiff dough is formed. Divide the dough into 14-15 walnut-size pieces. Roll into balls, then press down gently to flatten until about ½ inch thick. When you have shaped all the round cakes, cover them with a damp cloth to prevent them drying out.

Dust each flattened cake lightly with the extra flour and roll out to a circle about 3½ inches in diameter. It is easier to roll and fry one loochi at a time unless you have someone to help you. Do not stack the rolled loochis on top of each other as they will stick together.

Loochis puff up like balloons during frying. To ensure that the loochis are beautifully puffed, roll them out carefully and evenly without damaging or piercing them. Use a flat slotted spoon for frying.

Heat the oil to 325°F. Place one loochi at a time in the hot oil – it will soon float to the surface and start puffing up. To cook the loochi evenly, press it down gently by using the spoon only on the edge of the loochi. As soon as the loochi puffs up, turn it over gently and cook for about 30 seconds or until lightly browned. Drain on paper towels. Fry the rest of the loochis the same way. Keep the fried loochis in a single layer – do not pile one on top of the other as this will damage them.

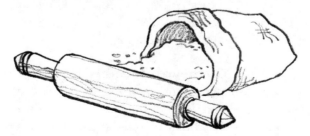

VEGETABLES

Many Indian people, and especially Hindus of higher castes, are vegetarian. The rich variety of vegetables that are grown in India allows for a most inventive and imaginative range of vegetable dishes within the classic cuisine of the country, a cuisine greatly influenced by religion.

Mushrooms, a Northern Speciality

Go to any Indian restaurant in the west and you are sure to find several dishes cooked with mushrooms on the menu as well as a mushroom bhaji, a side dish or vegetarian main course. It has therefore been a surprise for me to discover that mushrooms are certainly not a common vegetable in India, and that they are mainly grown in the north. The Mushroom Bhaji is something of a recent classic, a dish perhaps invented to appeal to the many westerners who now enjoy the rich variety of Indian foods. A classic Indian way of serving mushrooms would be in a curry as an appetizer or side dish, allowing the mushrooms to be savored for their own flavor.

Spinach – my Favorite Vegetable for Indian Cooking

There are many vegetables without which you simply cannot begin to make a good curry – onions and chilies immediately spring to mind, but for me one of the most versatile of vegetables is spinach. In the west we have the advantage of being able to purchase spinach chopped and frozen – so convenient for a side dish to be cooked in a hurry. "Saag" is the Indian term for spinach and Saag Bhaji is one of my favorite side dishes – I sometimes add a little flaked coconut if I serve it with a chicken curry as I find the flavors all blend well together. However, if you are cooking for a vegetarian, I thoroughly recommend the recipe for Palak Paneer (Paneer and Spinach) – paneer is a simple Indian cheese and adds plenty of protein to a vegetarian meal.

Know your Chilies – an Essential Indian Ingredient

So many Indian recipes call for chilies. When used fresh they are usually green and very hot – Indian chilies are long and thin; the fat, squat chilies available in supermarkets are milder and are more commonly associated with African cookery. Like all peppers, the chilies turn red as they ripen and become slightly less fiery in flavor and a little sweeter. The Indians, however, tend to use red chilies dried and this concentrates the flavor and the heat of the vegetable.

The hottest parts of the chili are the seeds around the core. Many Indians will cook with these to add extra fire to the dish but the seeds may be removed if a milder flavor is preferred. Cut the chilies in half lengthwise and scrape out the seeds. Chop the chili flesh very finely and remember to wash your hands very thoroughly immediately after dealing with them – rubbing my eyes with chili fingers is one of the most painful experiences I have ever had in the kitchen.

If you are just beginning to experiment with Indian cookery

you should go easy with the chilies. An old hand at Indian dishes will have built up a tolerance to the heat and may well like to add three or four chilies to a dish, whereas one or a maximum of two will be sufficient for the novice. Chilies, either as a vegetable or dried and ground as a spice, contribute the heat to Indian food. When cooking for friends it is advisable to err on the side of caution with the chilies – many people find it embarrassing if the curry is too hot for them to enjoy. Incidentally, milk is far more soothing than water if curry is too hot!

Potatoes – Vegetable or Snack Food?

Potatoes are one of the most successful vegetables for including in side dishes or for serving as a vegetable main course. They absorb flavors well and are delicious when cooked simply with fresh spices, for example fenugreek or cilantro leaves. They also combine well with other root vegetables to provide substantial vegetable main courses. Gobi Aloo, a lightly spiced dish of cauliflower and potatoes originating in northern India, must surely be one of the best known and most popular of vegetable combinations. However, I usually think of sweet potatoes when considering Indian vegetable dishes and it is interesting to note that, because of their sweet fragrant flavor (very similar to that of a parsnip), sweet potatoes are usually lightly fried and served as a savory snack rather than as part of a meal.

MIXED VEGETABLE CURRY

I find that my vegetable curries have a tendency to taste the same! Here green chilies are added toward the end of cooking for extra flavor and color.

Serves 4-6

INGREDIENTS
4-5 tbsps cooking oil
1 large onion, finely chopped
½-inch piece of fresh root ginger, peeled and finely sliced
1 tsp ground turmeric
1 tsp ground coriander
1 tsp ground cumin
1 tsp paprika pepper
4 small ripe tomatoes, skinned and chopped *or* a 7-ounce can of tomatoes with their juice
2 medium-size potatoes, peeled and diced
¼ pound string beans, sliced
2 medium-sized carrots, scraped and sliced
¾ cup garden peas, shucked weight
2 cups warm water
2-4 whole fresh green chilies
1 tsp garam masala
1 tsp salt
1 tbsp freshly chopped cilantro leaves

Heat the oil over medium heat and fry the onion until it is lightly browned. Add the ginger and fry for a further 30 seconds. Lower the heat and add the turmeric, coriander, cumin and paprika. Stir well. Add half the tomatoes and fry for 2 minutes, stirring continuously, then add all the other vegetables and the water. Mix well and bring to a boil, then cover and simmer for about 15-20 minutes until the vegetables are tender.

Add the remaining tomatoes and the green chilies to the curry. Cover and simmer for 5-6 minutes, then add the garam masala and salt, and mix well. Stir in half the cilantro leaves and remove the pan from the heat. Place the vegetable curry in a warmed serving dish and scatter the remaining cilantro leaves over the top.

CAULIFLOWER MASALA

Cauliflower Masala is a well flavored vegetable curry which is suitable for serving either as a main dish or as a vegetable accompaniment.

Serves 4-6

INGREDIENTS

1 cauliflower
2 potatoes
4 tbsps cooking oil
1 tsp cumin seeds
1 large onion, finely sliced
½ tsp ground turmeric
1 tsp ground coriander
1 tsp ground cumin
¼-½ tsp chili powder
2 ripe tomatoes, skinned and
  chopped
¾ cup warm water
1 cup shelled peas, fresh or
  frozen (cook fresh peas until
  they are tender before using)
1-2 fresh green chilies, de-seeded
  and slit lengthwise into halves
1 tsp salt
½ tsp garam masala
1 tbsp freshly chopped cilantro
  leaves

Cut the cauliflower into ½-inch flowerets – wash and drain. Peel and cut the potatoes lengthwise into ½-inch thick strips.

Heat the oil over medium heat and add the cumin seeds. As soon as they start to pop, add the onion and fry until it is soft. Lower the heat and add the turmeric, coriander, cumin and chili powder. Stir-fry for 2-3 minutes, then add the chopped tomatoes. Fry for a further 2-3 minutes, stirring continuously. Add the potatoes and the water. Bring to a boil, cover the pan and simmer for 6-8 minutes until the potatoes are half cooked. Add the cauliflower, cover the pan again and simmer for about 10 minutes, until the potatoes are tender.

Stir in the peas, green chilies, salt and garam masala. Cover the pan and cook for a further 5 minutes. Remove from the heat and stir in the cilantro leaves, then serve immediately.

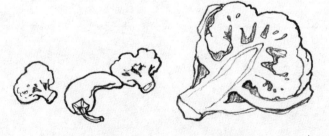

KHUMBI AUR BESAN KI BHAJI (MUSHROOMS WITH GRAM FLOUR)

Mushrooms are not all that common in India, but there are a few glorious mushroom dishes that are among my personal favorites. I always find that mushrooms provide a good color contrast in an Indian meal.

Serves 4

INGREDIENTS
- ¾ pound white mushrooms
- 2 tbsps cooking oil
- 2-3 cloves garlic, peeled and crushed
- ½ tsp salt
- ½ tsp chili powder
- 2 tbsps freshly chopped cilantro leaves
- 1 tbsp lemon juice
- 2 tbsps besan (gram flour or garbanzo bean flour), sifted

Wash the mushrooms and chop them roughly.

Heat the oil over medium heat and add the garlic. Allow it to brown slightly, then add the mushrooms. Stir and cook for 2 minutes. Add the salt, chili powder and cilantro leaves. Cook for 1 minute, then add the lemon juice and mix well. Sprinkle the besan over the mushroom mixture, and stir to mix immediately. Add extra salt if necessary and serve.

CABBAGE WITH CINNAMON

A most unusual combination of ingredients producing a delicious, mildly spiced side dish. A handful of frozen peas may be added for extra color.

Serves 4-6

INGREDIENTS
4 tbsps cooking oil
1 large onion, finely sliced
2 fresh green chilies, sliced lengthwise; de-seeded if a mild flavor is preferred
3 cinnamon sticks, 2 inches long, broken up into 2-3 pieces
1 large potato, peeled and cut into 1-inch dice
½ tsp ground turmeric
¼ tsp chili powder
½ cup warm water
1 small white cabbage, finely shredded
1 tsp salt
1 tbsp freshly chopped cilantro leaves

Heat the oil over medium heat and fry the onion, green chilies and cinnamon sticks until the onion is soft. Add the potatoes, and fry over low heat for 6-8 minutes. Stir in the turmeric and chili powder, and add the water. Bring it to a boil, cover the pan and simmer for 6-8 minutes, until the potatoes are half cooked. Add the cabbage and salt, and mix well. Lower the heat to the minimum, cover the pan and cook until the vegetables are tender (the cabbage should not be mushy). The finished dish should be fairly moist but not wet. If there is too much liquid left in the pan, remove the lid and let the liquid evaporate. Stir in the cilantro leaves, add extra salt if necessary and serve.

POTATOES WITH POPPY SEEDS

Poppy seeds do not only provide texture to dishes – they also add a delicate but distinctive flavor.

Serves 4-6

INGREDIENTS
5 tbsps cooking oil
½ tsp kalonji (onion seeds) (optional)
1 tsp cumin seeds
4-6 cloves garlic, peeled and crushed
1 tsp freshly ground black pepper
½ tsp ground turmeric
6 medium-size potatoes, peeled and diced
1 fresh green chili, finely chopped
6 tbsps white poppy seeds
1 tsp salt

Heat the oil to smoking point in a non-stick or cast iron skillet. Remove the pan from the heat and add the kalonji (if using) and cumin seeds. As soon as the seeds start crackling, add the garlic and return the pan to medium heat. Add the ground black pepper and turmeric. Stir briskly, then add the potatoes and green chili. Fry for 2-3 minutes, stirring constantly. Lower the heat, cover the pan and cook for 12-15 minutes, until the potatoes are tender, stirring occasionally.

Meanwhile, roughly grind the poppy seeds in a pestle and mortar or coffee grinder. Add to the potatoes. Raise the heat to medium and fry the potato and poppy seed mixture for 5-6 minutes, stirring frequently. Stir in the salt and serve immediately.

GREEN BEANS IN GARLIC BUTTER

This is a winning combination of ingredients and the dish is sure to be popular with everyone.

Serves 4-6

INGREDIENTS

2 tbsps sweet butter
½ tsp cumin seeds
3-4 cloves garlic, peeled and crushed or finely chopped
¼-½ tsp chili powder
1 pound whole green beans, fresh or frozen
½ tsp salt

Melt the butter over low heat and fry the cumin seeds for 30 seconds. Add the garlic and fry for 1 minute, then add the chili powder and the beans. Stir-fry for 1-2 minutes. Add the salt and mix thoroughly. Cover the pan and simmer the beans for 10-12 minutes in their own juice until they are tender, stirring occasionally. Serve immediately.

CAULIFLOWER WITH MUSTARD SEED

*I often serve cauliflower with a mustard sauce – this
cauliflower side dish is spiced with mustard seeds.*

Serves 4-6

INGREDIENTS
1 large cauliflower
6 tbsps vegetable oil
1 tbsp whole black mustard
  seeds
2 tsps whole fennel seeds
1 tsp whole cumin seeds
¼ tsp turmeric
4 cloves garlic, peeled and finely
  chopped
1 tsp salt
2 fresh green chilies, finely
  chopped
Cold water

Cut the cauliflower into small
flowerets, then wash and drain
them. Heat the oil in a large,
heavy based skillet over medium
heat. When hot, add the mustard,
fennel and cumin seeds. Once
the mustard seeds start to pop,
add the turmeric, garlic, salt and
chili and stir-fry until lightly
browned. Add a few tablespoons
of water and the cauliflower
flowerets Cook for about 5
minutes, until the cauliflower is
cooked but still firm. Add extra
water if necessary. Serve
immediately.

ALOO GAJJAR
(POTATO AND CARROTS)

Potatoes and carrots make a good base for a vegetable curry and the flavor of the carrots is accentuated by adding a little lemon juice to the vegetables just before serving.

Serves 2-3

INGREDIENTS

¼ cup ghee *or* 2 tbsps oil
1 tsp cumin seeds
2 medium-size potatoes, peeled
   and cut into ½-inch dice
3 carrots, peeled and diced
1 tsp chili powder
1 tsp ground coriander
¼ tsp turmeric powder
Salt to taste
Juice of ½ lemon

Heat the ghee or oil in a large skillet and add the cumin seeds. When they start to pop, add the potatoes. Fry for 3-4 minutes, then add the carrots. Stir in the chili, coriander, turmeric powder and salt. Stir-fry the mixture for 1-2 minutes, then cover and cook on low heat for 8-10 minutes. Add just a little water to help cook the carrots. Pour the lemon juice over just before serving.

SAAG (SPINACH) BHAJI

This is my very favorite side dish – I use fresh spinach from the garden or frozen chopped spinach.

Serves 4-6

INGREDIENTS
6 tbsps cooking oil
½ tsp black mustard seeds
1 tsp cumin seeds
8-10 fenugreek seeds (optional)
1 tbsp curry leaves
2-3 cloves garlic, peeled and finely chopped
2-4 dried red chilies, roughly chopped
1 pound fresh leaf spinach *or* ½ pound frozen leaf spinach, finely chopped
1 tbsp ghee or sweet butter
1 large potato, peeled and diced
1 large onion, finely sliced
½ tsp ground turmeric
1 tsp ground cumin
½ tsp garam masala
¼-½ tsp chili powder
2-3 ripe tomatoes, skinned and chopped
1 tsp salt

Heat 2 tbsps of oil over medium heat and fry the mustard seeds until they pop. Add the cumin seeds, fenugreek (if using) and curry leaves with the garlic and red chilies. Allow the garlic to brown slightly. Add the spinach, and mix thoroughly. Cover and simmer for 15 minutes, stirring occasionally.

Melt the ghee or butter in a skillet over medium heat and brown the diced potatoes. Remove from the heat and set to one side.

Heat the remaining oil over medium heat and fry the onion until well browned, taking care not to burn it as it will taste bitter if over-cooked. Lower the heat to minimum and add the turmeric, cumin, garam masala and chili powder. Stir-fry for 2-3 minutes. Add the spinach, potatoes, tomatoes and salt. Cover and simmer for 10 minutes or until the potatoes are tender, stirring occasionally. Remove from heat, add extra salt if necessary and serve.

LIMA BEANS AND GREEN BELL PEPPER

Lima beans and green bell pepper combine to give a most unusual, light, buttery flavor to this dish. It is dry, with next to no sauce, so it is ideal for serving as a side dish with a curry that has plenty of sauce.

Serves 4

INGREDIENTS
1 tbsp oil
1 onion, chopped
8-ounce can lima beans *or* ½ pound kidney beans
1 large green pepper, de-seeded and chopped
¼ tsp turmeric
½ tsp chili powder
1 tsp ground coriander
Salt
4-5 fresh or canned tomatoes, chopped
1 green chili, chopped
1 tbsp freshly chopped cilantro leaves

Heat the oil and fry the onion for 3-4 minutes. Add the beans and green pepper, and cook for 4-5 minutes. Stir in the turmeric, chili and ground coriander. Add salt to taste and then the tomatoes. Mix well. Cover and cook for 5-6 minutes over low heat, then add the green chili and fresh cilantro. Cook, covered, for 2-3 minutes. If the mixture is too dry, add 2 tbsps water.

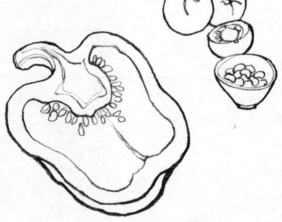

STUFFED PEPPERS

Stuffed peppers are an unusual Indian side dish, colorful and delicious.

Serves 6-8

INGREDIENTS

¼ cup ghee *or* 3 tbsps oil
1 onion, finely chopped
1 potato, peeled and diced
½ pound mixed frozen
  vegetables
1 tsp garam masala
½ tsp chili powder
2 tsp dried mango powder
Salt
6-8 small green bell peppers
Oil for frying

Heat the ghee or oil and fry the onion until soft. Add the potato and cook for 4-5 minutes, then add the mixed vegetables, and garam masala, chili powder, mango powder and salt to taste. Cover and cook gently until potatoes are soft, then remove from the heat and let cool.

Wash and dry the green bell peppers. Remove the tops by slicing across to form a lid. Remove the pith and seeds. Heat 3 tbsps of oil in a skillet and fry the peppers, laid sidewise, for 1-2 minutes, cooking them on all sides. Drain well. Stuff each pepper with filling and place on a baking sheet. Bake in a 325°F oven for 20 minutes, then serve.

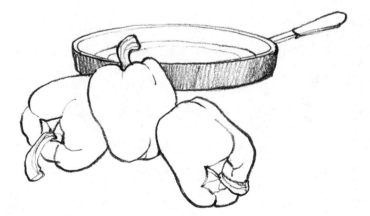

BHAREY BHINDI (WHOLE STUFFED OKRA)

The okra are really spiced, not stuffed, and served with a tasty onion dressing.

Serves 4-6

Ingredients
½ pound bhindi (okra), washed, dried, topped and tailed
4 tbsps ghee or oil
1 large onion, thickly sliced
2 tsp ground coriander
2 tsp ground cumin
1 tsp turmeric powder
1 tsp chili powder
Salt
1 tbsp dry mango powder
1 tbsp aniseed (sauf) powder

Split the okra or bhindi halfway down. Melt 1 tbsp of ghee or oil in a pan over medium heat, add the onion and cook for 30 seconds. Set to one side. Mix the coriander, cumin, turmeric and chili powder, and put a little of this spice mixture into the split okras. Heat the remaining ghee or oil in a skillet or wok, and add the stuffed okras. Sprinkle with salt and stir well. Cover and cook slowly for 5-6 minutes. Add the fried onion, and sprinkle with the mango and aniseed powder. Cover and cook for 3-4 minutes.

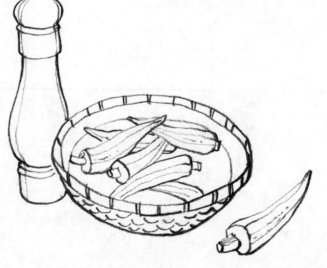

TENDLI BHAJI WITH CASHEW NUTS

Tendli is an Asian vegetable which tastes like zucchini but looks like a gooseberry. Use zucchini if tendli is not available.

Serves 4

INGREDIENTS
2 tbsps oil
⅓ cup cashew nuts
3-4 cloves of garlic, peeled and crushed
½ tsp mustard seeds
6-8 curry leaves
2-3 dry red chilies or fresh green chilies
½ pound tendli, washed, dried and cut in half lengthwise
Salt
2 tsps flaked coconut
¼ tsp turmeric powder

Heat the oil and fry the cashew nuts until lightly browned. Remove with a slotted spoon, then fry the garlic in the same oil until lightly browned. Add the mustard seeds, curry leaves and red or green chilies and fry for 30 seconds. Add the tendli, sprinkle with salt and stir. Add the flaked coconut, turmeric and fried cashew nuts. Cover and cook slowly for 10-12 minutes, or until the tendli is tender.

VEGETABLE NIRAMISH

This mixed vegetable curry is ideal for vegetarians, or for serving as a side dish with a meat or chicken curry. Use a selection of fresh vegetables in season.

Serves 4

INGREDIENTS
1 small eggplant
Salt
3 tbsps vegetable oil
1 onion, sliced
1 green chili, de-seeded and finely chopped
1 tsp cumin seeds
1 large potato, peeled and cut into chunks
¼ pound cauliflower flowerets
1 small green pepper, de-seeded and sliced
2 small carrots, peeled and thickly sliced
1 tsp ground coriander
1 tsp turmeric
1 tsp chili powder
⅔ cup vegetable stock
1 tsp freshly chopped cilantro leaves
Juice of 1 lime
Fresh chilies to garnish

Cut the eggplant into chunks and sprinkle liberally with salt, then let stand for 30 minutes. Rinse well and drain. Heat the oil in a pan and fry the onion, green chili and cumin seeds for 2 minutes. Stir in the potato and fry for 3 minutes. Add the eggplant, cauliflower, pepper and carrots and fry for a further 3 minutes. Stir in the spices and fry for 1 minute, then add the stock. Cover and simmer gently for 30 minutes until all the vegetables are tender, adding a little more stock if necessary. Add the cilantro and lime juice and simmer for 2 minutes. Serve garnished with fresh chilies.

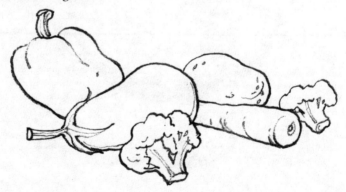

EGG & POTATO DUM

I love curried eggs and find them a wonderful dish to prepare when time and money are short.

Serves 4-6

INGREDIENTS
6 hard-boiled eggs
5 tbsps cooking oil
4 medium-size potatoes, peeled and quartered
Pinch of turmeric
Pinch of chili powder
1 large onion, finely chopped
½-inch piece of fresh root ginger, peeled and grated
1 cinnamon stick, 2 inches long, broken into 2-3 pieces
2 brown cardamoms, the top of each pod split open
4 whole cloves
1 fresh green chili, chopped
7-ounce can tomatoes
½ tsp ground turmeric
2 tsps ground coriander
1 tsp ground fennel
¼-½ tsp chili powder (optional)
1 tsp salt
1 cup warm water
1 tbsp freshly chopped cilantro leaves

Shell the eggs and make 4 slits lengthwise through each egg white, taking care not to cut right to the top or the bottom. Heat the oil in a cast iron or non-stick pan over medium heat (enamel or steel pans will cause the eggs and the potatoes to stick). Fry the potatoes until they are well browned on all sides, then remove them with a slotted spoon and set to one side. Remove the pan from the heat and stir in the turmeric and chili. Return the pan to the heat and fry the whole eggs until they are well browned. Remove them with a slotted spoon and set to one side. Fry the onion, ginger, cinnamon, cardamom, cloves and green chili in the same oil, until the onions are lightly browned. Add half the tomatoes. Cook until the tomatoes break up, then add the turmeric, ground coriander, fennel and chili powder (if using). Stir and cook for 3-4 minutes. Add the rest of the tomatoes and cook for 4-5 minutes, stirring frequently. Return the potatoes to the pan with the salt and water. Bring to a boil, cover the pan tightly and simmer until the potatoes are tender, stirring occasionally. Add the eggs and simmer, uncovered, for 5-6 minutes, stirring once or twice. Stir in the cilantro leaves, and serve.

MUSHROOM BHAJI

Anyone who visits Indian restaurants might think that mushrooms are a popular Indian ingredient but this is not so. Mushroom Bhaji, one of the most popular of vegetable side dishes, has really been developed for the western restaurant trade.

Serves 4

INGREDIENTS
3-4 tbsps cooking oil
1 onion, finely chopped
2-3 cloves garlic, peeled and
  crushed
½ tsp ground turmeric
½ tsp chili powder
1 tsp ground coriander
1 tsp ground cumin
¾ tsp salt
1 tbsp tomato paste
½ pound mushrooms, chopped

Heat the oil over medium heat and fry the onion until it is lightly browned. Lower the heat and add the garlic, turmeric, chili powder, coriander and cumin. Stir-fry the spices, adding about 1 tbsp of water to prevent them from sticking to the base of the pan. As soon as this water dries up, add a little more. Continue doing this until you have fried the spices for about 5 minutes.

Add the salt and tomato paste to the pan, then add the mushrooms. Stir until thoroughly mixed, then add about 2 tbsps of water and cover the pan. Simmer for 10 minutes. The finished dish should have a small amount of gravy but it should not be too wet. Reduce any excess liquid by fast boiling before serving the bhaji.

EGGPLANT BHARTA

A bharta is a dish of puréed or mashed vegetables, spiced for extra flavor.

Serves 4

INGREDIENTS

1 large eggplant weighing about 1 pound
4 tbsps cooking oil
½ tsp black mustard seeds
½ tsp fennel seeds
1-inch piece of fresh root ginger, peeled and grated
2-3 cloves garlic, peeled and crushed
1 fresh green chili, finely chopped
1 large onion, finely chopped
½ tsp ground turmeric
¼-½ tsp chili powder (optional)
2 small ripe tomatoes, skinned and chopped
1 tsp salt
½ cup freshly chopped cilantro leaves
1 small tomato, sliced

Wash the eggplant and make 2-3 small incisions in it to prevent it from bursting during cooking. Broil the eggplant for 12-15 minutes or until tender. Turn it frequently during cooking. Remove the eggplant and let it cool. Cut the eggplant lengthwise into two. Scrape out the flesh with a knife or spoon and discard the skin. Purée the flesh in a food processor or mash it with a fork.

Heat the oil over medium heat and add the mustard seeds. As soon as they begin to pop, add the fennel seeds, ginger, garlic and green chili. Stir-fry the ingredients for 1 minute, then add the onion. Fry the onion until it is just soft, then stir in the turmeric and chili powder. Add the tomatoes and cook for 2 minutes, then stir in the eggplant and salt, and cook for 2-3 minutes. Add half the cilantro leaves and remove the pan from the heat. Place the eggplant bharta in a warmed serving dish and garnish with the sliced tomato. Scatter the remaining cilantro leaves on top.

BHINDI (OKRA) MASALA

I love okra – they have a delicate yet distinctive flavor which is enhanced by light or medium spicing. Try to choose small, even-size okra for this recipe.

Serves 4

INGREDIENTS
½ pound bhindi (okra)
2 tbsps cooking oil
1 tsp ground coriander
¼ tsp ground cumin
½ tsp garam masala
¼ tsp ground turmeric
7-ounce can tomatoes
¼ tsp chili powder
½ tsp salt
1 tbsp freshly chopped cilantro
leaves

Scrub each bhindi gently, wash them and slice off the tops. Heat the oil over medium heat in a wide shallow pan. When hot, remove the pan from the heat to avoid burning the spices, and add the ground coriander, cumin, garam masala and turmeric. Return the pan to the heat and add the tomatoes and the chili powder. Stir and cook for 2-3 minutes, then add the whole bhindis and the salt. Stir and cover the pan. Lower the heat to the minimum and cook for about 10 minutes. Stir once or twice during this time. When cooked, the bhindi should be tender but still firm. Place the bhindi in a warmed serving dish and scatter the cilantro leaves on top.

CABBAGE WITH GRAM FLOUR

Cabbage, fresh spinach and kale may all be used with equal success in this quickly prepared dish.

Serves 4-6

INGREDIENTS
4 tbsps cooking oil
½ tsp black mustard seeds
½ tsp cumin seeds
8-10 fenugreek seeds
3-4 cloves garlic, peeled and crushed
Pinch of asaphoetida (optional)
1 onion, finely shredded
¼ tsp ground turmeric
½ tsp chili powder
2½ cups finely shredded white cabbage
1 tsp salt
¼ cup water
2 tbsps besan (gram flour or garbanzo bean flour), sifted

Heat the oil in a wide shallow pan over medium heat and fry the mustard seeds until they pop. Add the cumin seeds and the fenugreek, then stir in the garlic and allow it to brown slightly. Add the asaphoetida (if using) and the onion, turmeric and chili powder. Stir-fry for 1-2 minutes, then add the cabbage and salt, and mix thoroughly. Lower the heat, cover the pan and cook for 8-10 minutes, stirring occasionally. The cabbage should be cooked but still slightly crisp. Sprinkle the water evenly on the cabbage, then sprinkle on the besan and cook for 1-2 minutes, stirring continuously. Serve immediately.

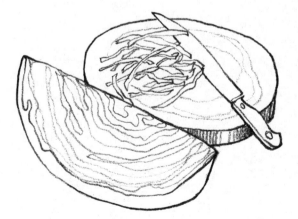

ALOO MATTAR
(POTATOES AND PEAS)

Potatoes are often used as the main ingredient for side dishes and are served in the same way as any other vegetable – with rice or breads.

Serves 4-6

INGREDIENTS

4 tbsps cooking oil
1 onion, finely chopped
2 cinnamon sticks, 2 inches long, broken up
½-inch piece of fresh root ginger, peeled and finely chopped
½ tsp ground turmeric
2 tsps ground cumin
¼ tsp chili powder
¼ tsp freshly ground black pepper
4 medium-size potatoes, peeled and cut into 1-inch cubes
1-2 whole fresh green chilies
1 tbsp tomato paste
1 tsp salt
1 cup warm water
1 cup frozen peas
1 tbsp freshly chopped cilantro leaves (optional)

Heat the oil over medium heat and fry the onion, cinnamon and ginger for 4-5 minutes, stirring frequently. Lower the heat and add the turmeric, cumin, chili powder and black pepper. Stir-fry for 1 minute. Add the potatoes and green chilies, and cook for 2-3 minutes until the spices are thoroughly blended. Stir in the tomato paste and salt, then add the water. Bring to a boil, cover the pan and cook over medium to low heat for 10 minutes, until the potatoes are half cooked. Add the peas, cover the pan and cook until the potatoes are tender. Remove the pan from the heat, stir in half the cilantro leaves (if using) and scatter the remainder on top.

BHINDI (OKRA) WITH COCONUT

Many people find the texture of okra to be a little too smooth – the poppy and sesame seeds in this recipe add extra texture, even after they have been ground.

Serves 4

INGREDIENTS

½ pound bhindi (okra)
2 tbsps sesame seeds
1 tbsp white poppy seeds
2 tbsps flaked coconut
1-2 dried red chilies
1 fresh green chili, roughly chopped
3 tbsps cooking oil
½ tsp black mustard seeds
¼ tsp fenugreek seeds
2 cloves garlic, peeled and finely chopped or crushed
½ tsp salt

Wash the bhindi, trim off the stalks and cut each bhindi into two pieces. Heat an iron griddle or heavy based pan over medium heat and dry roast the sesame and poppy seeds until they are lightly browned. Transfer the seeds to a plate and let them cool. Reheat the griddle and dry roast the coconut until lightly browned, stirring constantly. Transfer the coconut to a plate and let it cool.

Roughly grind the sesame, the poppy seeds, and the dried red chilies in a coffee grinder or pestle and mortar. Add the coconut and fresh green chili and grind until smooth. Heat the oil over medium heat and add the mustard seeds. As soon as the seeds start to pop, add the fenugreek and garlic. Let the garlic brown slightly, then add the bhindi and salt. Stir and mix thoroughly. Lower the heat to the minimum, cover the pan and cook for about 10 minutes, stirring occasionally. Stir in the ground ingredients and mix well. Remove from the heat, add extra salt if necessary and serve immediately.

SPICED GREEN BEANS

Green beans make wonderful Indian side dishes – if you grow them yourself you will welcome this recipe for using up your surplus produce.

Serves 4-6

INGREDIENTS
2 tbsps sesame seeds
3 tbsps cooking oil
¼ tsp black mustard seeds
4-6 cloves garlic, peeled and finely chopped
1-2 dried red chilies, roughly chopped
½ tsp ground turmeric
1 tsp ground coriander
1 pound frozen sliced green beans, defrosted and drained, or fresh in season
¾ tsp salt
1 tbsp flaked coconut

Heat an iron griddle or heavy based pan over medium heat and dry roast the sesame seeds until they are lightly browned, stirring constantly. Transfer them to a plate and let cool. Heat the oil in a pan over medium heat and add the mustard seeds. When they begin to pop, add the garlic and let it brown slightly. Add the red chilies, turmeric and coriander, stir briskly and add the beans and salt. Mix thoroughly. Lower the heat to the minimum, cover the pan tightly and cook until the beans are tender, stirring occasionally. This will take 15-20 minutes. Grind the sesame seeds and the coconut in a pestle and mortar or a coffee grinder and stir them into the beans. Season with extra salt if necessary and serve.

KASHMIRI DUM ALOO (SPICED POTATOES WITH YOGURT)

New potatoes are fried until brown and then dressed with yogurt and spices in this delicious vegetable dish. The green chili is added as a garnish at the end of cooking.

Serves 4

INGREDIENTS
1¼ pounds small new potatoes
1 tbsp ghee or sweet butter
1 tsp fennel seeds

Ground Spices
½ tsp ground cumin
1 tsp ground coriander
¼ tsp freshly ground black
  pepper
½ tsp ground turmeric
½ tsp ground ginger

⅔ cup thick plain yogurt
1 tsp salt
¼ tsp garam masala
1 tbsp freshly chopped cilantro
  leaves
1 fresh green chili, de-seeded
  and finely chopped

Boil the potatoes in their skins. Let them cool, then peel. Prick the potatoes all over with a cocktail stick to enable the spices to penetrate deep inside. Melt the ghee or butter over medium heat in a non-stick or cast iron pan (steel or enamel pans will cause the potatoes to stick and break up). When it is hot, fry the potatoes in a single layer until they are well browned, turning them over frequently. Remove them with a slotted spoon and set aside.

Remove the pan from the heat and stir in the fennel seeds and the ground spice mixture. Turn the heat to low and place the pan back on the heat. Stir the spices and fry for 1 minute. Add the yogurt and salt. Mix well, then add the potatoes, cover the pan and simmer for 10-12 minutes. Add the garam masala and remove the pan from the heat. Stir in the cilantro leaves and the green chili and serve.

STRING BEAN AND
POTATO BHAJI

*String beans and potatoes – two of my favorite side dish
vegetables combined in a wonderfully flavored bhaji*

Serves 4-6

INGREDIENTS
4-5 tbsps cooking oil
½ tsp black mustard seeds
½ tsp cumin seeds
1 large onion, finely sliced
3-4 dried red chilies, roughly
chopped
10-12 fenugreek seeds
½ cup freshly chopped cilantro
leaves,
½ tsp ground turmeric
1 large potato, peeled and cut
into matchsticks
¾ pound string beans, sliced
1 tsp salt
1 tsp ground cumin

Heat the oil over medium heat
and add the mustard seeds. As
soon as the seeds start to pop,
add the cumin seeds, onions, red
chilies and fenugreek. Fry for
3-4 minutes, stirring frequently.
Add the cilantro leaves and
turmeric, and fry for 1 minute.
Add the potatoes, beans and salt.
Stir until the ingredients are
thoroughly mixed. Cover the pan
and cook on low heat for about
25 minutes, until the vegetables
are tender, stirring occasionally.
Add the ground cumin, cook for
a further 2-3 minutes, then serve.

POTATOES WITH GARLIC AND CHILIES

A spicy shallow-fried Indian vegetable – perfect for serving with plainly cooked meat or fish.

Serves 4-6

INGREDIENTS

1 pound potatoes, peeled
3 tbsps cooking oil
½ tsp black mustard seeds
½ tsp cumin seeds
4 cloves garlic, peeled and crushed
¼-½ tsp chili powder
½ tsp ground turmeric
1 tsp salt

Cut the potatoes to the thickness of short French fries. Heat the oil over medium heat in a wide, shallow non-stick or cast iron pan. Add the mustard seeds and cumin. When the seeds start popping, add the garlic and let it brown lightly. Remove the pan from the heat and add the chili powder and turmeric, then add the potatoes and return the pan to the heat. Stir and raise the heat to medium. Add the salt. Stir and cover the pan, then cook for 3-4 minutes and stir again. Continue cooking and stirring until the potatoes are cooked and lightly browned. Serve immediately.

GOBI MATTAR (CABBAGE WITH GARDEN PEAS)

I always think of peas as the perfect accompaniment to lamb and therefore recommend serving this with any lamb curry. The dish is more colorful if you use a green cabbage rather than white.

Serves 4-6

INGREDIENTS

¾ pound green cabbage
3 tbsps cooking oil
¼ tsp black mustard seeds
½ tsp cumin seeds
10-12 fenugreek seeds (optional)
2-4 dried red chilies, whole
1 small onion, finely sliced
½ tsp ground turmeric
1 cup frozen peas
¾ tsp salt
1 tsp ground coriander
¼-½ tsp chili powder
2 small ripe tomatoes, skinned and chopped
1 tbsp freshly chopped cilantro leaves (optional)

Shred or chop the cabbage finely. Heat the oil over medium heat and fry the mustard seeds until they pop. Add the cumin seeds, fenugreek (if using), red chilies and onions. Stir-fry until the onions are soft. Stir in the turmeric and add the cabbage. Mix thoroughly, then add the peas and salt. Cover the pan, lower the heat and cook for 5 minutes. Add the ground coriander, chili powder and the chopped tomatoes. Stir-fry until completely dry.

Remove the pan from the heat and stir in half the cilantro leaves. Turn the cabbage into a warmed serving dish and garnish with the remaining cilantro leaves.

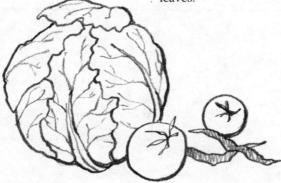

ALOO KI BHAJI
(SPICED POTATOES)

*I always enjoy the combination of potatoes and onions,
enhanced in this dish by whole spices and chilies.*

Serves 4-6

INGREDIENTS

1½ pounds potatoes
5-6 tbsps cooking oil
½ tsp black mustard seeds
2-3 dried red chilies
⅛ tsp fenugreek seeds
2 medium-size onions, finely
    sliced
1-2 fresh green chilies, sliced
    lengthwise and de-seeded if a
    mild flavor is preferred
1 tsp ground turmeric
1 tsp salt
1 cup freshly chopped cilantro
    leaves

Boil the potatoes in their skins,
then let them cool thoroughly.
Peel the potatoes and dice them
evenly.

Heat the oil over medium heat in
a wide shallow pan and fry the
mustard seeds until they pop.
Add the red chilies and the
fenugreek seeds, then the onions
and green chilies. Fry until the
onions are golden brown. Add
the turmeric, potatoes and salt.
Stir-fry gently until the potatoes
are heated through, then add the
cilantro leaves and serve.

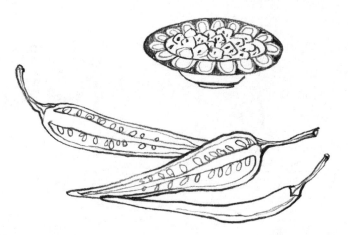

ALOO-MATTAR AND MIRCHI BHAJI (POTATO, PEA AND GREEN PEPPER CURRY)

This potato and pea curry is unusual as it also includes green pepper – this makes it refreshingly different!

Serves 4

INGREDIENTS

1 onion, chopped
¼ cup ghee *or* 2 tbsps oil
2 potatoes, peeled and diced
1 tsp ground coriander
1 tsp chili powder
¼ tsp ground turmeric
2 cups frozen peas
1 green pepper, de-seeded and
  cut into pieces
7-ounce can chopped tomatoes
Salt
2 green chilies, cut into quarters
1 tbsp freshly chopped cilantro
  leaves
½ cup water

Fry the onion in the ghee or oil until softened, then add the potatoes and fry for 5-6 minutes. Add the ground coriander, chili powder and turmeric. Mix well and add the peas and green bell pepper. Stir, add the tomato and season with salt. Add the chopped green chilies, fresh cilantro and water. Cover and cook for 5-6 minutes until the potatoes are tender.

GOBI ALOO (CAULIFLOWER & POTATOES)

This is a truly classic Indian side dish, and one of the best known. Slow cooking with spices gives a subtle but distinctive flavor.

Serves 4-6

INGREDIENTS

3 potatoes
1 cauliflower
5 tbsps cooking oil
½ tsp black mustard seeds
½ tsp cumin seeds
12-15 fenugreek seeds
1-2 dried red chilies, roughly chopped
1 onion, roughly chopped
1 fresh green chili, roughly chopped
½ tsp ground turmeric
½ tsp ground cumin
1 tsp ground coriander
1¼ tsps salt
1 tbsp freshly chopped cilantro leaves (optional)

Boil the potatoes in their skins and let them cool thoroughly. Peel the potatoes and cut them into 2-inch dice. Blanch the cauliflower in boiling water for 2 minutes. Do not over-boil as it should remain firm after cooking. Let the cauliflower cool and then cut it into ½-inch flowerets.

Heat the oil over medium heat in a wide shallow pan, preferably non-stick or cast iron. Add the mustard seeds, and as soon as they begin to pop, add the cumin and fenugreek seeds and the red chilies. Add the onion and the green chili. Stir-fry until the onion is golden brown. Add the cauliflower, lower the heat, cover the pan and cook for 6-8 minutes. Add the potatoes, turmeric, cumin, coriander and salt. Stir gently until all the ingredients are thoroughly mixed. Cover the pan and cook for 5-6 minutes until the potatoes are heated through. Stir in the cilantro leaves and serve immediately.

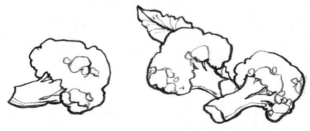

GREEN BEAN BHAJI

For best results use frozen beans for this bhaji – the ice will help to make just the right amount of liquor for serving with the beans.

Serves 4

INGREDIENTS
3 tbsps oil
1 tsp urid dhal
2-3 green chilies
6-8 fresh curry leaves
¾ pound frozen sliced green beans
Salt to taste
1 tbsp flaked coconut

Heat the oil and add the urid dhal, green chili and curry leaves. Stir-fry for a half minute, then add the beans and sprinkle with salt. Cover and cook for 6-8 minutes. Add the coconut and mix well. Cover and cook for 3-4 minutes. Serve with chapatis.

TOORAI TARKARI
(ZUCCHINI CURRY)

This is a tasty side dish at any time of the year but is especially good to make when zucchini and tomatoes are plentiful.

Serves 4

INGREDIENTS

1½ tbsps oil
1 tsp cumin seeds
½ pound zucchini, peeled and
  sliced into ¼-inch circles
½ tsp chili powder
1 tsp ground coriander
¼ tsp turmeric powder
3-4 fresh or canned tomatoes,
  chopped
Salt to taste
1 green chili, halved
1 tbsp freshly chopped cilantro
  leaves

Heat the oil and add the cumin seeds. When they start to pop, add the zucchini slices. Stir and add the ground chili, coriander and turmeric powder. Mix well and add the chopped tomatoes, salt, green chili and fresh cilantro. Cover and cook for 10-12 minutes. Add extra salt if necessary and serve immediately.

KHATA-MEETHA KADDU (SWEET AND SOUR PUMPKIN)

Pumpkin is a very versatile vegetable. It stays moist during cooking, allowing this to be a moist curry although it has no sauce.

Serves 4

INGREDIENTS

4 tbsps ghee *or* 3 tbsps oil
1 bay leaf
1 inch cinnamon stick
6 green cardamoms
6 cloves
1 tsp five-spice mixture (panchphoran)
2 potatoes, peeled and diced
1 pound pumpkin, peeled and diced
1 tsp chili powder
1½ tsps ground coriander
¼ tsp ground turmeric
½ tsp salt
2 tsps sugar
1 tbsp tamarind pulp
3 tbsps water

Heat the ghee or oil and add the bay leaf, cinnamon, cardamoms, cloves and five-spice mixture. Fry for 30 seconds. Add the potatoes and fry for 4 minutes, then add the pumpkin. Stir the vegetables and cook for 3 minutes. Add the chili powder, coriander, turmeric, salt and sugar. Stir, then add the tamarind pulp and water. Cover and cook over gentle heat for 8-10 minutes, until the potatoes are tender.

PALAK PANEER
(PANEER AND SPINACH)

Paneer is an Indian cheese. If unavailable, use Feta in its place – you will need a cheese that will fry and not melt.

Serves 4

INGREDIENTS
1 pound fresh spinach leaf *or* ½ pound defrosted frozen chopped spinach
4 tbsps ghee *or* 3 tbsps oil
½ pound paneer, diced
1 onion, finely chopped
1-inch piece fresh root ginger, peeled and finely chopped
4 fresh tomatoes *or* 4-5 canned tomatoes, chopped
1 tsp chili powder
1 tsp ground coriander
¼ tsp ground turmeric
¼ tsp salt
1 tbsp lemon juice
2 tbsps sweet butter

Boil the fresh spinach in the water for 5 minutes. Drain and reserve the water. Chop or purée the spinach and set to one side. If thawed frozen spinach is used, save the liquid.

Heat the ghee or oil in a large pan and fry the paneer pieces until lightly browned. Remove with a slotted spoon and put to one side. In the same oil, fry the onion and ginger for 3-4 minutes. Add the tomatoes, then the chili, coriander, turmeric and salt to taste. Cover and cook for 2-3 minutes. Add the paneer, puréed spinach and lemon juice. If the mixture is too dry, add 2-3 tbsps spinach water to moisten the curry. Remove from heat and serve with butter.

ALOO METHI
(POTATO AND FRESH
FENUGREEK LEAVES)

This vegetable side dish is best made with fenugreek leaves but cilantro leaves could be used as a substitute.

Serves 3-4

INGREDIENTS
4 tbsps ghee *or* 3 tbsps oil
1 tsp cumin seeds
1 pinch asafoetida (hing)
3 potatoes, peeled and cut into chunks
1 bunch fresh fenugreek (methi) leaves, chopped
1 tsp chili powder
1 tsp coriander powder
Salt
¼ tsp turmeric powder
Juice of 1 lemon

Heat the ghee or oil in a large skillet and add the cumin seeds and asafoetida. When the seeds start to pop, add the potatoes. Fry for 3-4 minutes, then add the fenugreek leaves. Mix well and add the chili powder, coriander, salt and turmeric, stirring well. Cover and cook over a low heat for 6-8 minutes. Add the lemon juice before serving.

SALADS, SAUCES & RELISHES

The classic Indian way of serving salad vegetables is raw in side dishes, providing a contrast to meat and vegetables dishes cooked and served in rich sauces. How dull an appetizer of popadoms and relish would be without a simple salad of tomato and onion to serve with it.

Indian markets are the most colorful of places, to both the eye and the nose! Spices, essential to all Indian dishes, are sold from sacks amidst piles of fresh herbs and a staggering array of colorful fruits and vegetables. Many of the vegetables make refreshing salads, but some may require a little explanation for the novice curry cook.

Mooli – Peppery but Mild

A salad vegetable widely available in most western supermarkets but perhaps requiring a little explanation is the mooli – a long white radish, also known as "daikon" in Oriental cooking. It is pungent when cut – especially when grated, as this allows much of the juice to flow freely – but the actual flavor is surprisingly mild. The white flesh of the mooli provides a stunning color contrast to brightly colored vegetables such as carrots, and the mild, slightly peppery flavor blends well with just about every salad vegetable – I love it with watercress, but that is not a classic Indian combination! A word of warning – store grated mooli in an air-tight box in the refrigerator; plastic wrap is rather too permeable to confine the aroma.

An Essential in any Meal

Pickles and relishes add so much extra flavor to Indian meals; they might be spicy relishes or cooling sauces depending on the ingredients used. They were traditionally home-made, but the marvellous range of authentic pickles and relishes that is now commercially available, combined with a different life-style for the Indian women of today, means that relatively few people still make these at home. However, raitas – mild yogurt sauces flavored with salad vegetables and served as an accompaniment to many spicy dishes and fried appetizers – are best when home-made on the day that they are to be eaten.

No-cook Dressings for the Perfect Finishing Touch

Raitas are like the vast majority of salads – they generally involve no cooking and are just a mixing together of various ingredients. A few spices may occasionally require roasting to enhance their flavor before being added to the yogurt, but that is often all the cooking there is to do. Cucumber, carrot and onion raitas are all made in this way but there are some interesting variations which do actually require the vegetables to be cooked – recipes for potato, okra and eggplant raitas are included in this chapter and are well worth the preparation required for a special Indian meal – the texture of fried vegetables within a raita is delicious.

Quick-cook Relishes

There is quite a difference between a relish and pickles in Indian cooking – relishes are usually mild and pickles, often cooked in oil, vary between hot and exceptionally hot and should be treated with the utmost respect!

The relishes included here are mild and fragrant, often little more than sauces. They add lightness and freshness to an Indian meal. Two of them really set my taste buds tingling! The Avocado Relish recipe is very similar to a Mexican guacamole but without the garlic and tomato. A little heat is provided by the chopped green chili but the overall taste sensation is mild and creamy, and the relish is delicious with chicken dishes and dhals. Green Cilantro Relish combines all the brightness and fragrance of cilantro leaves with the delicate flavor of coconut and the traditional Indian seasonings of garlic, chilies and ginger. Try to buy the cilantro leaves in a specialist Indian store – a small package of leaves from the supermarket will be very expensive, although, I have to say, in my opinion the taste justifies the cost!

Most of the relishes included in this chapter are for immediate consumption but any left-overs may be kept in the refrigerator for a few days, or as specified in the recipe. The Red Hot Relish, and others requiring long cooking and storage to allow them to mature, should be preserved in clean glass jars, dried in a warm oven and filled when both the jars and the relish are hot. Always cover relishes with screw tops and not cellophane tops – this prevents any evaporation from the relish, which may lead to it drying out during storage.

195

KACHHOOMAR (SHREDDED ONION SALAD)

Cut the onion into rings for the most attractive presentation of this salad. I serve this with popadoms and relishes as an easy appetizer.

Serves 4

INGREDIENTS
1 large Spanish onion, finely sliced
¼ tsp salt
¼ tsp chili powder
1 tbsp freshly chopped cilantro leaves
1 green chili, chopped
1 tbsp lemon juice
2 fresh tomatoes, chopped (optional)

Place all the ingredients in a bowl and toss together to mix. Leave for 10 minutes, so that the juice from the onion starts to run, then serve with kebabs, curries or pakoras.

196

CARROT AND COCONUT SALAD

*Coconut is often used in curries – the association of carrots
with Indian food is less obvious. This salad is light and
refreshing – the perfect accompaniment to the hotter curries
such as vindaloos.*

Serves 4-6

INGREDIENTS
1½ cups grated carrots
2 tbsps flaked coconut
2 tbsps finely shredded onion
1 tbsp lemon juice
2 tbsps freshly chopped cilantro
    leaves
1 fresh green chili, de-seeded
    and roughly chopped
    (optional)
½ tsp salt

Combine all the ingredients
except the salt in a bowl. Stir in
the salt just before serving.

KASSI MOOLI
(GRATED MOOLI)

A simple salad, but one with a strong aroma! Mooli actually taste quite mild but have a very distinctive fragrance – wrap the salad well or store in an air-tight box and keep it in the refrigerator.

Serves 4

INGREDIENTS
½ pound mooli
Salt
Juice of 1 lemon
1 green chili, finely chopped
1 tbsp freshly chopped cilantro
  leaves

Wash and peel the mooli, then grate it. Place the grated mooli in a sifter, press lightly and allow some of the liquid to drain away, then transfer the mooli to a serving dish.

Sprinkle the mooli with salt and lemon juice and mix in the chili and cilantro.

NARANGI PIYAZ SALAD (ONION AND ORANGE SALAD)

This side salad is delicious – a refreshing and unusual blend of flavors. Use corn oil or vegetable oil for the dressing.

Serves 4

INGREDIENTS
2 large seedless oranges *or* 4
  tangerines
6 finely chopped scallions,
  including the green leaves
Salt
2 tsps lemon juice
¼ tsp freshly ground black
  pepper
½ tsp sugar
2 tsps salad oil

Peel the oranges and cut or break them into segments – cut the segments into two if they are large. Add the scallions, salt, lemon juice, pepper, sugar and oil. Toss the salad gently, combining the oranges and onions with the dressing.

CABBAGE AND MINT SALAD

The mint sauce used in this salad gives it a vivid color and strong flavor.

Serves 4-6

INGREDIENTS

3 cups finely shredded white cabbage
1 small onion, finely chopped
1 fresh green chili, finely chopped, de-seeded if a mild flavor is preferred
2-3 tbsps thick plain yogurt
2 tsps mint sauce
½ tsp salt

Put the finely shredded cabbage in a large mixing bowl. Add the rest of the ingredients and mix thoroughly. Place the salad in a serving dish, cover and chill before serving.

TOMATO AND CUCUMBER SALAD

This makes a colorful side dish to serve with almost any curry. The peanuts add color and texture to the salad.

Serves 4-6

INGREDIENTS

½ cucumber
2 tomatoes
1 bunch scallions, roughly chopped
1 tbsp lemon juice
1 tbsp olive oil
¼ tsp salt
¼ tsp freshly ground black pepper
1 tbsp freshly chopped cilantro leaves
¼ cup crushed roasted salted peanuts

Peel the cucumber and chop it finely. Chop the tomatoes finely, then place the cucumber, tomatoes and scallions into a serving bowl.

Combine the lemon juice, olive oil, salt, pepper and cilantro leaves and set to one side. Combine all the ingredients just before serving.

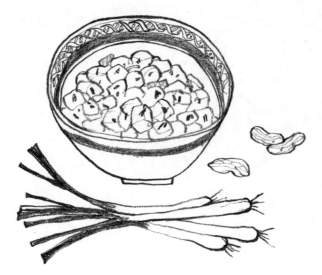

SMOKED MACKEREL SALAD

Smoked mackerel works well in this salad, which would be made with home-smoked fish in India. The marinated fish may be served on small savory crackers as a cocktail snack.

Serves 4

INGREDIENTS
½ pound smoked mackerel
½ cup finely chopped onions
1 fresh green chili, de-seeded and finely chopped
2 tbsps freshly chopped cilantro leaves
1½ tbsps lemon juice

Remove the skin and bones from the fish and flake the flesh with a fork. Add all the remaining ingredients and mix thoroughly. Cover and refrigerate for 2-3 hours. Serve with a green salad.

CARROT AND MOOLI
SALAD

Mooli, a white radish, is now widely available in supermarkets and specialist shops. This makes an excellent side dish to serve with any but the creamiest curries.

Serves 4-6

INGREDIENTS
1 tbsp cooking oil
½ tsp black mustard seeds
½ tsp cumin seeds
⅔ cup coarsely grated carrots
1⅓ cups coarsely grated mooli
½ tsp salt
2-3 tbsps finely chopped onion
1 tbsp lemon juice
1 tbsp finely chopped cilantro
  leaves

Heat the oil over medium heat and fry the mustard seeds until they pop. Add the cumin and remove from heat. Add the grated carrots and mooli and let cool. Stir in the salt, onion, lemon juice and cilantro leaves before serving.

POTATO RAITA

In this unusual raita lightly cooked potato is cooled before being added to spiced yogurt.

Serves 4-6

INGREDIENTS
2 tbsps cooking oil
¼ tsp fennel seeds
1 clove garlic, peeled and finely chopped
2 medium-size potatoes, peeled and diced
½ tsp ground cumin
½ tsp salt
⅔ cup plain yogurt
½ tsp sugar
¼ tsp chili powder or paprika pepper

Heat the oil over medium heat and fry the fennel seeds until they are brown. Add the garlic and let it turn slightly brown, then add the potatoes and stir. Cover the pan and cook until the potatoes are soft and brown, stirring frequently. Stir in the cumin and salt, mix thoroughly and remove from the heat. Let cool completely.

Beat the yogurt and sugar until smooth. Add the spiced potatoes with any oil that remains in the pan. Stir and mix well. Place the raita in a serving dish and sprinkle with the chili powder or paprika before serving.

CUCUMBER RAITA

This is a very mild, refreshing raita, lightly spiced with roasted cumin seeds.

Serves 4-6

INGREDIENTS
1 small cucumber
1 tsp cumin seeds
⅔ cup thick plain yogurt
¼ tsp salt
¼ tsp paprika pepper

Peel the cucumber and cut lengthwise into two halves. Slice each half finely. Heat a small pan over low heat and dry roast the cumin seeds until they turn a shade darker. Let the seeds cool, then crush them with a rolling pin or in a pestle and mortar.

Beat the yogurt until smooth, then stir in the cumin with the salt. Reserve a few slices of cucumber for garnish and add the rest to the yogurt. Mix thoroughly. Place the raita in a serving dish and arrange the reserved cucumber on top. Sprinkle the paprika evenly over the sliced cucumber.

BHINDI (OKRA) RAITA

Fried bhindi are crispy and not sticky – the texture of stewed okra can be off-putting. This is an unusual, spicy raita.

Serves 6-8

INGREDIENTS
Oil for deep-frying
½ pound bhindi (okra), cut into
    very thin slices
½ tsp salt
1 fresh green chili, de-seeded
    and roughly chopped
⅔ cup thick plain yogurt
½ tsp mustard powder
1 tbsp cooking oil
½ tsp black mustard seeds
1 tbsp curry leaves

Deep-fry the bhindi until they are well browned and crispy. Drain on paper towels, then let cool completely.

Add the salt to the green chili and crush to a pulp. Beat the yogurt with a fork until smooth, then add the mustard powder and the green chili mixture. Stir and mix well. Gently stir in the fried bhindi.

Heat the 1 tbsp oil in a small pan and fry the mustard seeds until they crackle. Add the curry leaves and fry for 15-20 seconds. Remove the pan from the heat and stir the seasoned oil into the bhindi raita with all the seasonings. Serve lightly chilled.

MINT AND ONION RAITA

This raita may be made with dried mint, but I prefer to use fresh garden mint.

Serves 4-6

INGREDIENTS
⅔ cup thick plain yogurt
1 small onion, finely chopped
1 tbsp freshly chopped fresh
  mint or dried mint
1 fresh green chili, de-seeded
  and chopped
½ tsp salt
¼ tsp paprika pepper

Beat the yogurt until smooth. Add the remaining ingredients, except the paprika, and beat again. Place the raita in a serving dish and sprinkle with the paprika before serving.

CARROT AND PEANUT RAITA

A colorful and highly nutritious raita, ideal for serving with vegetable curries.

Serves 4-6

INGREDIENTS
2 carrots
⅓ cup roasted salted peanuts
1 small clove of garlic, peeled and roughly chopped
1 fresh green chili, de-seeded and roughly chopped
¼ tsp salt
⅔ cup thick plain yogurt
½ tsp sugar
1 tbsp freshly chopped cilantro leaves

Peel and grate the carrots coarsely. Crush the peanuts with a pestle and mortar or a rolling pin. Mix the garlic, chili and salt and crush to a pulp.

Beat the yogurt until smooth and stir in the garlic mixture. Add the carrots, peanuts, sugar and cilantro leaves and mix thoroughly. Chill and serve.

CUCUMBER AND ONION RAITA

This is one of the most popular, and cooling, raitas or yogurt sauces. Add more or less onion, to taste.

Serves 4-6

INGREDIENTS
1 tsp cumin seeds
⅔ cup plain yogurt
3 tbsps finely chopped onion
½ cucumber, peeled and finely
  chopped
½ tsp salt

Heat a cast iron or heavy based pan and dry roast the cumin seeds until they release their aroma. Let cool; then crush them lightly in a pestle and mortar.

Beat the yogurt with a fork until smooth, then add the remaining ingredients and half the crushed cumin seeds. Mix thoroughly. Place the raita in a serving dish and scatter the remaining cumin seeds on top.

EGGPLANT RAITA

*All raitas are quite cooling – they are good to have to offer if
your curry is hotter than planned! Cook the eggplant for the
full 10 minutes or the flesh will be difficult to mash.*

Serves 6-8

INGREDIENTS

1 eggplant weighing about ¾
  pound
½ tsp salt
½-inch piece of fresh root ginger,
  peeled and roughly chopped
1 fresh green chili, roughly
  chopped and de-seeded for a
  mild flavor
⅔ cup thick plain yogurt
2-3 tbsps finely chopped onion
2 tbsps freshly chopped cilantro
  leaves

Make one or two small incisions
in the eggplant to prevent it from
bursting during cooking.

Broil the whole eggplant for 10
minutes, turning it over once. Let
it cool completely.

Add the salt to the ginger and
green chili and crush them to a
pulp. Cut the eggplant
lengthwise into two halves and
scoop out the flesh. Chop the
flesh finely or mash it. Beat the
yogurt until smooth. Add the
ginger and chili pulp and mix
well. Add the eggplant and mix
thoroughly. Stir in the onion and
half the cilantro leaves just
before serving. Garnish with the
remaining cilantro.

DATE SAUCE

This is a sweet and sour relish to serve with kebabs, pakoras or any snack. Tamarind is easiest to use in concentrate form.

Serves 6-8

INGREDIENTS
½ cup pitted dates
2 tbsps seedless raisins
1 tsp ground cumin
1 tsp chili powder
1 tsp tamarind concentrate *or* 3
   tbsps lemon juice
¾ tsp salt
1 tsp dark brown sugar, packed
½ cup cold water

Place all the ingredients in a blender, except half the water. Mix until the ingredients are half blended, then add the remaining water and mix until fairly smooth. Pour the sauce into a sifter and press it through with a metal spoon until only a dry and coarse mixture is left in the sifter. Discard this mixture and transfer the sauce to a serving bowl.

ONION RELISH

*I often find raw onions too strong, so I suggest washing the
onions for this relish before adding them to the
other ingredients.*

Serves 4-6

INGREDIENTS

2 cups finely chopped onions
1 fresh green chili, de-seeded
  and finely chopped
1 tbsp finely chopped fresh mint
1 tbsp finely chopped fresh
  cilantro
1 tbsp lemon juice
½ tsp salt

Mix all the ingredients together
except the salt. Add the salt just
before serving. This will prevent
the relish from becoming too wet
before it is served.

GREEN CILANTRO
RELISH

How did we enliven our food before cilantro leaves were widely available? This glorious relish celebrates the fresh flavor of cilantro.

Serves 6-8

INGREDIENTS

¾ cup water
⅓ cup flaked coconut
1-2 fresh green chilies, chopped, de-seeded if a mild flavor is preferred
1-2 cloves garlic, peeled and roughly chopped
½-inch piece of fresh root ginger, peeled and roughly chopped
30g/1oz freshly chopped cilantro leaves .
½ tsp salt
1 tbsp lemon juice

Bring the water to a boil. Remove it from the heat and soak the coconut in the water for 10-15 minutes. Place all the ingredients in a blender or food processor and mix until smooth. Let cool completely.

AVOCADO RELISH

I love the creamy rich flavor of avocado. It blends easily with garlic, chili and cilantro leaves to make a delicious sauce or relish.

Serves 6-8

INGREDIENTS

1 ripe avocado
Juice of ½ lemon
¼ cup plain cottage cheese
1 clove garlic, peeled and
  chopped
2 tbsps freshly chopped cilantro
  leaves
1 fresh green chili, chopped,
  de-seeded if a mild flavor is
  preferred
½ tsp salt

Cut the avocado into two and remove the pit. Scoop out the flesh. Place the lemon juice in a blender or food processor and add the avocado with all the remaining ingredients. Blend until smooth, adding a little water if necessary. Taste, add a little extra salt if necessary, and chill until required.

APPLE RELISH

This fruity relish is quite highly spiced and makes a perfect accompaniment to all Indian snacks and appetizers. Store the relish in the refrigerator.

Serves 8-10

INGREDIENTS
1 tbsp cooking oil
½ tsp black mustard seeds
¼ tsp fenugreek seeds
¼ tsp ground turmeric
Pinch of asaphoetida (optional)
2 large cooking apples, peeled and finely chopped
½-¾ tsp chili powder
1½ tsps salt
3 tbsps light brown sugar, packed

Heat the oil over medium heat and fry the mustard seeds until they pop. Add the fenugreek, turmeric and asaphoetida, then the apples. Stir and mix thoroughly. Add the chili powder, salt and sugar. Stir and cook until the apple starts to soften. Cover and simmer until the apple is tender, stirring frequently. Let the relish cool. Store in a screw-top jar in the refrigerator for 4-6 weeks if not used immediately.

CUMIN-CORIANDER
RELISH

This is a mild relish to serve with pakoras or any appetizer or snack. The raw onions are actually dominated by the spices, especially the cumin.

Serves 4-6

INGREDIENTS

1 tsp cumin seeds
1 tsp coriander seeds
2-3 dried red chilies
4 tbsps flaked coconut
¼ cup water
½ tsp salt
1½ tbsps lemon juice
2-3 tbsps finely chopped onion

Grind the cumin, coriander, red chilies and coconut in a pestle and mortar or a coffee grinder until the ingredients are smooth. Transfer to a bowl and add the water, salt and lemon juice. Mix thoroughly, then stir in the finely chopped onion.

MINT AND ONION RELISH

*This is a light relish, more like a marmalade. It will keep for
several weeks in an air-tight container or jar in
the refrigerator.*

Serves 6-8

INGREDIENTS
2 tbsps cooking oil
1 large onion, roughly chopped
A few sprigs fresh mint
1 fresh green chili, de-seeded if a
  mild flavor is preferred
1 tbsp lemon juice
½ tsp salt

Heat the oil over medium heat and fry the onion until soft but not brown. Let cool. Place the onion and the rest of the ingredients in a blender or food processor and mix until smooth. Store in an air-tight container or screw-top jar in the refrigerator.

MEETHI TOMATAR RELISH (SWEET TOMATO RELISH)

This tomato relish is only lightly spiced and quite delicious.
Store any surplus in the refrigerator in sealed jars.

INGREDIENTS
2 tbsps ghee *or* 1 tbsp oil
1 inch cinnamon stick
1 bay leaf
6 cloves
1 tsp mustard seeds
1 tsp chili powder
¼ tsp turmeric powder
¼ cup sugar
1 pound fresh or canned
  tomatoes
⅓ cup raisins
½ tsp salt

Heat the ghee or oil and fry the cinnamon, bay leaf and cloves for 1 minute. Add the mustard seeds. When they start to pop, add the chili, turmeric and sugar. Mix well and add the tomatoes. Mix again and add the raisins and salt. Cover and simmer for 8-10 minutes. Add a little water if necessary.

ADRAK KHAJOOR KI KHATI MITHI RELISH (DATE AND GINGER RELISH)

This sweet, spicy relish is ideal with meat or chicken curries. It may be preserved and kept for up to 3 months, in or out of the refrigerator.

INGREDIENTS
⅔ cup sliced and pitted dates
1-inch piece fresh root ginger, peeled and cut into matchsticks
¼ pound fresh, unripe mango, peeled and thinly sliced *or* 2 ounces dry mango pieces (aamchur)
⅓ cup raisins
¼ cup chopped almonds
1 cup water
¾ cup sugar or grated jaggery
¼ tsp salt
1 tsp chili powder

Place the dates, ginger, fresh or dry mango, raisins and almonds in a pan, and add the water. Leave for 6-8 minutes. Add the sugar or grated jaggery, salt and chili powder and bring gently to a boil. Simmer for 15-20 minutes until the relish is thick and sticky. Remove, cool and serve.

TMALI KI RELISH
(TAMARIND RELISH)

Tamarind Relish goes really well with kebabs. It keeps in the refrigerator for up to a month. Tamarind is a sticky paste or pulp – the tamarind is sometimes called the Indian date. You will find it in specialist Indian shops.

Serves 6-8

INGREDIENTS
½ pound dry tamarind pods
½-¾ cup sugar or grated jaggery
¼ tsp salt
1 tsp chili powder
1 tsp cumin seeds
1 tsp coriander seeds

Soak the tamarind pods in ½ cup of boiling water for 5 minutes. Squeeze the pods to remove the soft pulp. Strain through a sifter or squeeze dry by hand. Add a little fresh warm water to the pulp and repeat the process 3 times. Discard the pods. The first extract will be the thickest and subsequent ones will be thinner and milder. Take 1 cup of the tamarind liquid. Add the sugar or jaggery, salt and chili powder. Lightly roast the cumin and coriander seeds in a dry skillet and cook over low heat until lightly browned. Grind the spices, add to the tamarind mixture and mix well. Adjust the sugar and salt if necessary.

NAU-RATTAN RELISH
(NINE JEWELLED RELISH)

This is a relish to preserve and keep, and to use as required.
It is quite thick and sticky.

INGREDIENTS
1 banana, sliced
1 apple, cored and chopped
1 large mango, peeled, pitted and sliced
3 rings of canned pineapple, chopped
½ pound canned peaches, drained and chopped
⅔ cup pitted and sliced dates
1 inch fresh root ginger, peeled and chopped
⅓ cup raisins
¾ cup brown sugar or jaggery
2-3 dry red chilies
¾ cup malt vinegar
1 tsp salt
½ tsp cumin seeds
½ tsp coriander seeds
½ tsp onion seeds
½ tsp aniseed seeds
½ cup chopped almonds

Put all the fruits, dates, ginger, raisins, sugar, chilies and malt vinegar in a large pan. Add the salt and simmer gently for 10-15 minutes.

Put all the whole spices in a dry skillet and cook over low heat until lightly browned. Let cool and then grind in a pestle and mortar. Add the coarsely ground spices and the almonds. Mix well and cook for 5-6 minutes. Cool slightly and store in screw-top jars.

LAL MIREH AUR MOONG PHALI RELISH (RED-HOT RELISH)

This relish can be as "red-hot" as you like – add more or less red chilies to taste! The red pepper gives lots of color to the dish and the peanuts add texture.

Serves 4

INGREDIENTS
1 large red pepper
3-4 whole dried red chilies
⅓ cup unsalted peanuts
½-inch piece fresh root ginger, peeled and sliced
Juice of 3 lemons
Salt

Cut the red pepper in half, remove the pith and seeds. Put it in a blender or food processor with the chilies, peanuts and ginger and mix until smooth. A few spoonfuls of lemon juice may be needed to blend the mixture. Pour into a bowl. Add the salt and the lemon juice, mix well and serve.

DAHI-PODINA RELISH (YOGURT AND MINT RELISH)

This is a very simple relish or raita to serve with any number of curries. Ready-made mint sauce may be used in place of fresh or dried mint.

Serves 4

INGREDIENTS
1¼ cups plain yogurt
4 tsps sugar
1 tbsp freshly chopped mint *or* 2 tsps dried mint powder
Salt

Place the yogurt, sugar and mint in a blender or food processor and mix for 1-2 minutes. Add the salt and mix.

DESSERTS & DRINKS

Desserts are not all that common in India – sweetmeats and sweet dishes are eaten but more as snacks during the day than as the final course of a meal. However, for banquets and feast days Indians delight in sweet dishes, which in wealthy households are often lavishly decorated with edible gold or silver leaf.

Any Excuse is a Good Excuse

A new baby, exam results, a visitor, someone going away – any excuse is a good excuse for a celebration and sweetmeats are the real celebratory foods of India. They are occasionally made at home but the markets are full of stalls selling fudges, halvas, and other milk-based delicacies. Modern stores sell such foods clinically packaged but most people would prefer to seek out the traditional experts in this field, the *halvais*, who sell their goods from stalls or open-fronted shops in the markets. Many sweetmeats are time-consuming and complicated to prepare, so Indian logic says leave them to the experts!

Rich and Creamy Milk Puddings

Most of the milk used in Indian cooking is full fat and when I have made Indian desserts at home I have found that the best results are achieved using full-fat milk. The milk is often boiled for a considerable time to evaporate some of the whey, leaving an even thicker, richer liquid. For convenience, the recipes for halva and firni in this chapter use canned evaporated milk. Other recipes actually specify full-fat milk and you should be certain to use this to achieve the correct consistency and the best possible result.

Indian milk puddings often contain nuts, and pistachios are particularly popular, for both their flavor and color. Cardamom seeds are the most common spice used in sweet dishes but the more typical flavorings for desserts are light and fragrant – flower waters are widely used.

Vermicelli and rice are both used extensively in desserts but the resulting puddings are usually served cold – in most other cuisines rice or macaroni puddings would be served hot. These puddings are more highly spiced than many others and, indeed, they rely on the spices for any flavor that they have. Puddings which are mainly milk and semolina or ground almonds are popular in India but seldom appeal to western tastes.

Fabulous Exotic Fruits

Mangoes, pineapples, bananas and coconuts – fruits that sound exotic to us are commonplace in India and are frequently eaten either by themselves or made into sorbets or sherbets. There is absolutely no comparison between a fruit such as a mango which is grown, ripened and eaten in the same country and a fruit that is picked and then transported halfway round the world, slowly ripening under refrigeration. One of my favorite desserts in this chapter is Melon Balls in Mango Purée – the combination of flavors is exceptional but both fruits need to be fully ripe to produce the best results.

Halva, a Popular Indian Sweetmeat

I have always thought of halva as a sweetmeat made from sesame seeds and originating in the Middle East. However, the Indians make what they call halva from a milk-based mixture, often flavored with vegetables such as carrots as well as nuts and sugar. The recipe for Carrot Halva is particularly popular and it is traditionally served as part of a celebratory meal, decorated with edible gold leaf, whereas the Semolina and Almond Halva is more suitable for everyday eating.

Refreshing Drinks of Fruit or Spice

The most famous of all Indian drinks must surely be tea (see recipe for Spiced Tea) but many other drinks are made from fruits or spices. There is also an up-and-coming brewing industry and Indian beers are now widely available in western supermarkets – most people prefer to drink beer with Indian food rather than wine. The very popular southern Indian drink of Rasam is made from a lightly spiced infusion of red lentils and is served warm – a far cry from a traditional western lemon soda or fruit juice! Rasam is usually served as a drink although some may prefer to present it as a thin soup which may be sipped throughout a meal.

Most fruit drinks require chilling for at least two hours before serving – I find this is especially important when serving drinks based on mangoes. A mango as a fruit at room temperature is refreshingly juicy and delicious. Served as a drink at the same temperature it is dull and insipidly sweet.

CARROT HALVA

Halva is very sweet and very popular. This recipe for carrot halva is most unusual.

Serves 6

INGREDIENTS
6 cups grated carrots
2 cups evaporated milk
⅔ cup sugar
1-inch piece cinnamon stick
2 bay leaves
½ cup blanched almonds, chopped
½ cup sweet butter
8 green cardamoms, de-seeded and crushed
¼ cup chopped pistachio nuts

Place the carrots, milk and sugar in a heavy based saucepan, with the cinnamon stick and bay leaves. Cook over low heat, until the liquid has almost completely evaporated. Stir in the almonds, butter and cardamom seeds. Continue cooking over low heat, stirring continuously, until the mixture in the pan changes color from orange to a deep red or brown. This may take up to 40-45 minutes.

Drain off any oil which may appear, and spread the halva mixture onto a flat dish. Serve hot or cold, sprinkled with the pistachio nuts.

SWEET SAFFRON RICE

This is a sweet pilaf, cooked using sugar instead of salt! Wash the rice under running water until the water is clear.

Serves 8-10

INGREDIENTS
1 cup basmati rice
2½ cups hot water
1 cinnamon stick, 2 inches long, broken into 2 pieces
4 whole cloves
¼ tsp saffron strands
3 tbsps ghee or sweet butter
1 tsp ground cardamom
¼ tsp ground nutmeg
½ cup superfine sugar
⅓ cup raw cashews, split into halves
¼ cup raisins or golden raisins

Wash the rice and soak it in cold water for 30 minutes; drain thoroughly. Place the water, cinnamon, cloves and saffron in a pan and heat until boiling. Cover and leave to stand for 15 minutes.

Heat a large pan, add the ghee or butter and then add the rice. Fry for 3-4 minutes until it begins to look fairly dry. Stir frequently. Add the cardamom and nutmeg, stir and mix well. Add the sugar and the spiced liquid; then stir until the sugar is dissolved. Stir in the cashews and the raisins or golden raisins. Cover and simmer gently for 10-12 minutes, then stand off the heat for a further 2-3 minutes. Fork through the rice, remove the cinnamon and cloves and serve.

DURBARI MALPURA

*These are small pancakes covered in fruit, nuts and cream
and flavored with nutmeg and orange zest.*

Serves 6

INGREDIENTS
¾ cup all-purpose flour
2½ tbsps ground rice
¼ cup superfine sugar
1 tsp ground or finely grated
  nutmeg
Pinch of baking soda
Finely grated zest of 1 orange
2 tbsps lightly crushed raw
  cashews
2 tbsps lightly crushed walnuts
½ cup full-fat milk
Oil for deep-frying
1 tbsp butter
¼ cup golden raisins
¼ cup flaked almonds
1¼ cups light cream
1 tbsp rosewater

Put the flour, ground rice, sugar,
nutmeg, baking soda, orange zest
and crushed nuts in a bowl. Add
the milk and stir until a thick
batter is formed.

Heat the oil over medium heat in
a deep skillet. Add 1 heaped
teaspoon of the batter at a time
until the whole pan is filled with

a single layer. When the
malpuras (spoonfuls of batter)
start floating to the surface, turn
them over. Fry gently until
golden brown on both sides –
about 5 minutes. Drain on paper
towels.

Melt the butter over low heat and
fry the golden raisins for 1
minute. Remove them with a
slotted spoon and drain on paper
towels. Fry the almonds in the
same fat until they are lightly
browned. Drain on paper towels.
Place the cream in a pan large
enough to hold all the malpuras
and bring to a slow simmer. Add
the malpuras and stir gently.
Turn the entire contents of the
pan onto a warmed serving dish
and sprinkle the rosewater over
the top. Decorate with the fried
golden raisins and almonds.
Serve hot or cold.

VERMICELLI KHEER

Vermicelli are used in a number of popular Indian puddings. This one is lightly spiced and creamy.

Serves 6-8

INGREDIENTS

2 tbsps ghee or sweet butter
1 ounce plain vermicelli
¼ cup golden raisins
¼ cup blanched and slivered
  almonds
2½ cups full-fat milk
¼ cup sugar
1 tbsp ground almonds
½ tsp ground cardamom seeds
½ tsp ground cinnamon
1 tbsp rosewater *or* ½ tsp vanilla
  or almond flavoring

Melt the ghee or butter in a pan over low heat and add the vermicelli, golden raisins and slivered almonds. Stir-fry for about 2-3 minutes until the vermicelli are golden brown. Add the milk, sugar and ground almonds. Bring to a boil and simmer gently for 20 minutes, stirring frequently. Stir in the ground cardamoms and cinnamon and remove the pan from the heat. Let the kheer cool slightly, then stir in the rosewater or other flavoring. Serve hot or cold.

FIRNI (CREAMED GROUND RICE WITH DRIED FRUIT AND NUTS)

An aromatic rice pudding to serve hot or cold.

Serves 6-8

INGREDIENTS
1¼ cups fresh milk
¼ cup ground rice
1 tbsp ground almonds
14-ounce can evaporated milk
¼ cup sugar
1 tbsp rosewater
1 tsp ground cardamom seeds
¼ cup flaked almonds
¼ cup lightly crushed pistachio
  nuts
2 tbsps finely chopped dried
  apricot

Place the milk in a heavy based pan over medium heat. Mix the ground rice and ground almonds together and sprinkle evenly over the milk. Bring to a boil, stirring frequently. Add the evaporated milk and sugar. Stir and cook over low heat for 6-8 minutes. Remove the pan from the heat and let the mixture cool – stir occasionally to prevent a skin from forming. When cool stir in the rosewater and the ground cardamom.

Reserve a few almonds, pistachios and apricots. Stir the remainder into the pudding. Transfer the firni to a serving dish and top with the reserved fruit and nuts. Serve hot or cold.

231

SPICED MANGO FOOL

Ripe mangoes eaten in their native country taste completely different! However, this spiced fool makes the most of canned fruits.

Serves 6-8

INGREDIENTS
2 tbsps milk
¼ tsp saffron strands
6-ounce can evaporated milk
¼ cup sugar
1 tbsp fine semolina
2 tbsps ground almonds
1 tsp ground cardamom seeds
2 × 15-ounce cans mangoes,
  drained and puréed
1 cup cream cheese
¼ cup lemon juice

Put the milk into a small pan and bring to a boil. Stir in the saffron strands, remove from the heat, cover the pan and set aside. Put the evaporated milk and sugar in a pan over low heat. When it begins to bubble, sprinkle the semolina over the milk and stir until well blended. Add the ground almonds, stir and cook until the mixture thickens – this will take 5-6 minutes. Stir in the ground cardamoms and remove the pan from the heat. Let cool completely, then gradually beat in the mango purée, making sure there are no lumps.

In a large mixing bowl whip the cream cheese with the lemon juice, then gradually beat in the evaporated milk and mango mixture. Stir in the saffron milk with all the strands – these will continue to impart their color and flavor to the mango purée. Mix well. Spoon into a serving dish and chill for 2-3 hours.

RASMALAI

A classic Indian milk dessert, spiced with cardamoms which always cleanse the palate.

Serves 4

INGREDIENTS
4 pints milk
Lemon juice
2 tsps all-purpose flour
8 green cardamoms, crushed
2-3 sugar cubes, cut in 12 small
  pieces

Milk Sauce
2½ cup milk, reduced by boiling
  to 2 cups

Syrup
1½ cups granulated sugar
1¼ cups water

Decoration
¼ tsp rosewater or orange flower
  water
¼ cup chopped pistachio nuts
¼ cup chopped almonds

Bring the 4 pints of milk to a boil and add a little lemon juice. Leave to stand until separated. Cool for 10 minutes and then strain through a fine sifter or a clean piece of cheesecloth. Leave to drain overnight.

Boil the milk for the sauce to reduce, then prepare the sugar syrup. Combine the granulated sugar and water in a pan and cook over low heat for 2-3 minutes to dissolve the sugar. Bring to a boil and continue to boil for about 3 minutes or until syrupy.

Transfer the milk curds to a bowl and beat with an electric mixer or wooden spoon for about 5 minutes to soften. Add the flour and the cardamom seeds gradually, and continue beating. Leave for 2-3 minutes, then divide the mixture into 12. Place a piece of sugar cube in the centre of each portion, then press gently to flatten into 1½-inch circles.

Bring the sugar syrup back to simmering point and drop in the rasmalai balls, a few at a time. Boil them for 10 minutes. Place the milk sauce in a serving dish. Remove the rasmalai from the syrup with a slotted spoon and place them in the milk sauce. When all the rasmalai are cooked and in the milk sauce, sprinkle with rosewater or orange flower water and the chopped nuts. Let cool and then chill before serving.

MELON BALLS IN MANGO PURÉE

Melon and mango make a perfect partnership of flavors in this refreshing dessert.

Serves 6

INGREDIENTS
2 × 15-ounce cans of sliced
  mangoes
1 galia or honeydew melon
Finely grated zest of 1 lemon
2 tbsps superfine sugar
2 tbsps cornstarch
½ tsp ground nutmeg
⅔ cup heavy cream

Drain the canned mangoes and purée them in a blender or food processor or push them through a sifter. Using a melon baller make as many balls as possible out of the melon. Scoop out any remaining flesh and mix in a blender or food processor with any juice.

Transfer the melon purée to a pan and add the lemon zest and sugar. Blend the cornstarch with a little water and add to the melon purée. Cook over low heat until the mixture thickens. Stir in the nutmeg and remove from the heat. Let the mixture cool slightly, then mix it with the mango purée.

Whip the cream until thick, then stir it into the mango mixture. Pour the melon and mango mixture into a pie plate and arrange the melon balls around the edge. Chill for 2-3 hours before serving.

SHRIKAND

This rich and creamy dessert is made from strained yogurt –
you will need very fine cheesecloth to strain the
yogurt properly.

Serves 6

INGREDIENTS
3 × 15-ounce cartons of thick
   plain yogurt
¼ tsp saffron strands
1 tbsp hot water
⅓ cup superfine sugar
1 tbsp ground almonds
½ tsp ground cardamom seeds
¼ tsp grated or ground nutmeg

Pour the yogurt onto a clean,
very fine piece of cheesecloth;
bring together the four corners of
the cloth so that the yogurt is
held in the middle. Tie the four
corners into a tight knot and
hang the cheesecloth over the
sink until all the water content

has been drained off; this will
take 4-6 hours or can be done
overnight.

Add the saffron strands to the hot
water, cover and set aside.
Carefully untie the cheesecloth
and empty the contents into a
mixing bowl. Beat the strained
yogurt with a fork, or a wire
beater, until smooth. Add the
sugar and mix thoroughly. Add
the ground almonds, cardamom
and nutmeg and mix well. Stir in
the saffron strands and the water
in which it was soaked. Chill
before serving.

SPICED FRUIT SALAD

Most of the fruits required for this recipe are now available fresh, so you may use all fresh or a mixture of fresh and canned – whichever you prefer. Use apple juice if there is not enough syrup from the fruit.

Serves 6-8

INGREDIENTS
15-ounce can pineapple chunks
15-ounce can papaya chunks
15-ounce can mango slices, cut into chunks
15-ounce can guava halves, cut into chunks
3 cinnamon sticks, each 2 inches long
3 brown cardamoms
6 whole cloves
8 black peppercorns

Drain all the fruits and reserve the syrup. Mix all the syrups together and reserve 2½ cups Place the syrup in a pan and add the spices. Bring to a boil, cover the pan and simmer for 20 minutes. Remove the lid of the pan and reduce the syrup to half of its original volume by boiling for 5-6 minutes. Remove from the heat and let the syrup cool. Cover the pan while the syrup cools – in an open pan some of the flavor would be lost. Reserve a few pieces of papaya and guava and all the mango. Arrange the remaining fruits in a serving bowl. Arrange the mangoes on top, then add the reserved papaya and guava. Strain the spiced syrup and pour it over the fruits. Cover and chill before serving.

MANGO DELIGHT

I prefer to use fresh mangoes for this dessert, but only if they are really ripe. If not, use canned mangoes – but you may need to reduce the sugar in the recipe slightly to compensate for the sweetness of the syrup.

Serves 4-6

INGREDIENTS

2 fresh ripe mangoes *or* 2 × 15-ounce cans of sliced mangoes

2 tbsps cornstarch

2 tbsps sugar

½ tsp vanilla flavoring

⅔ cup milk

1 tsp ground cardamoms or mixed spice

⅔ cup heavy cream

2 tbsps lightly crushed shelled unsalted pistachio nuts

Drain one can of the mango slices and purée them in a blender or food processor. Drain the other can and coarsely chop the mango slices. If using fresh mangoes, peel and slice them. Mix the cornstarch and sugar together, and the vanilla, then gradually add the milk and blend well. Cook over low heat until the consistency resembles whipped cream, then stir in the ground cardamoms or mixed spice and remove from the heat. Gradually add the mango pulp, or the chopped flesh of one of the mangoes to the mixture, stirring all the time.

Whisk the cream until fairly thick, but still of a pouring consistency. If you buy extra thick heavy cream, there is no need to whisk it. Stir the cream into the mango mixture and gently mix in the remaining chopped mangoes. Transfer the mango mixture to a serving bowl and top with the crushed pistachio nuts. Serve hot or cold.

SEMOLINA AND ALMOND HALVA

*Halva is very rich and very sweet – serve only small pieces
and keep any remaining halva well chilled*

Serves 6-8

INGREDIENTS
½ cup ghee or sweet butter
⅔ cup fine semolina
⅔ cup ground almonds
½ cup sugar
½ tsp ground nutmeg
1¼ cups full-fat milk
¼ cup chopped raw cashews

Grease a large plate and set it to one side. Melt the ghee or butter in a pan over low heat. Add the semolina and cook for 6-7 minutes, stirring continuously until golden brown. Add the almonds, sugar and nutmeg, stir and mix thoroughly. Add the milk and mix, stirring until the mixture thickens and stops sticking to the base and sides of the pan.

Put the mixture onto the greased plate and spread it evenly to about ½ inch thickness; use the back of a lightly greased metal spoon to do this. Using a knife, press the sides inwards to form a large square. Sprinkle the chopped cashews evenly over the halva and press them in gently with the palm of your hand. Let the mixture cool and cut into 1-inch squares.

SWEET VERMICELLI

This dish is a Muslim speciality and is always made during the festival of "Idd Ul Fitr."

Serves 6

INGREDIENTS

¼ pound plain vermicelli
¼ cup ghee or sweet butter
¼ cup golden raisins
⅓ cup coarsely chopped raw cashew nuts
⅓ cup coarsely chopped blanched almonds
4 green cardamom pods, split open at the top
½ tsp ground cardamom seeds
½ tsp ground nutmeg
1¼ cups water
¼ cup sugar

Break the vermicelli into small pieces. Melt 1 tbsp ghee or butter over low heat and fry the golden raisins until they swell up. Remove the pan from the heat and transfer the golden raisins to a plate with a slotted spoon. Place the pan back over the heat, add all the nuts and stir-fry until the nuts turn slightly brown. Transfer them with a slotted spoon to another dish. Return the pan to the heat again and add the remaining ghee or butter. Turn the heat up to medium, add the whole cardamoms and fry for 30 seconds. Add the vermicelli and fry until it is a rich golden color, stirring constantly – this will take about 5 minutes.

Remove the pan from the heat. Add the golden raisins, half the fried nuts, the ground cardamom and the ground nutmeg and stir briskly. Return the pan to the heat and add the water and sugar. Bring to a boil, cover the pan and simmer for 5 minutes. Remove the lid, turn the heat to medium and cook the vermicelli for 2-3 minutes or until the liquid dries up, stirring constantly. Sweet Vermicelli may be served hot or cold. If serving cold, use a fork to separate the vermicelli strands as they will stick together when cold. Decorate with the remaining fried nuts.

COCONUT STUFFED PANCAKES

These lightly spiced pancakes are sure to be popular with all the family at any time of the year.

Makes 6 pancakes

INGREDIENTS
For the Filling
⅔ cup flaked coconut
¼ cup dark brown sugar, packed
2 tbsps lightly crushed walnut
   pieces
6-ounce can evaporated milk
1 tsp ground cardamom seeds

Mix all the ingredients, except the ground cardamom, in a small pan and cook over medium heat. As soon as the mixture begins to bubble, lower the heat and let simmer without a lid for 8-10 minutes, stirring occasionally. Stir in the ground cardamoms, remove the pan from the heat and let the mixture cool.

For the Pancakes
2 eggs
1½ cups whole wheat flour
1 tsp ground cinnamon
1 tbsp caster sugar
1 cup milk
Ghee or sweet butter for frying

Place all ingredients, except the ghee or butter, in a large bowl and beat with a wire whisk until smooth. This batter can also be prepared in a blender or food processor. Place a non-stick or cast iron skillet over low heat. When hot, melt a little ghee or butter on it, about ¼ teaspoon. Pour 2 tablespoons of the batter into the pan. Spread it quickly by tilting the pan. The pancake will set in a minute or so. Let it cook for a further minute, then carefully turn it over with a thin spatula, or toss it. Cook the other side for about 1 minute (brown spots should appear on both sides). Spread 1 tablespoon of the filling on one side of the pancake and roll it up. Make the rest of the pancakes in the same way.

KULFI
(INDIAN ICE CREAM)

*This is the most popular ice cream in India! It is firmer than
most ice creams and needs to be put in the refrigerator for
around 90 minutes before serving.*

Serves 6-8

INGREDIENTS
1¼ cups fresh milk
2 tbsps ground rice
1 tbsp ground almonds
14-ounce can evaporated milk
1 tsp ground cardamom seeds
¼ cup sugar
2 cups heavy cream
1 tbsp rosewater or 5-6 drops of
 any other flavoring, such as
 vanilla, almond etc.
⅓ cup lightly crushed shelled,
 unsalted pistachio nuts

Heat the milk until it is
lukewarm. Place the ground rice
and ground almonds in a small
bowl. Gradually add the warm
milk, a little at a time, to make a
thin paste of pouring
consistency. Stir continuously to
break up any lumps. If any
lumps remain, sift the mixture.

Bring the evaporated milk to a
boil and add the ground
cardamom. Take the pan off the
heat and gradually add the
almond and rice mixture, stirring
continuously. Add the sugar and
cream and place the pan over a
medium heat. Cook the mixture
for 12-15 minutes, stirring
continuously. Remove the pan
from the heat and let the mixture
to cool slightly. Add the
rosewater or other flavoring and
half of the pistachio nuts, stir and
mix well. Let the mixture cool
completely, stirring frequently to
prevent a skin from forming on
the surface.

When the mixture has cooled
completely, put it into a plastic
ice cream box or individual
molds. Top with the remaining
pistachio nuts and put in the
freezer for 4-5 hours. Move the
kulfi to the refrigerator for 1½
hours before serving. This will
soften it slightly and make it
easier to cut. The time required
to soften the kulfi will vary
according to the size of the
container used for freezing.

STUFFED LYCHEES

*Lychees grow throughout India and are a popular dessert –
simply as ripe fruit enjoyed on its own. It is easier to use
canned lychees if you want to stuff the fruits – they are
pitted before canning and are therefore much easier
to prepare.*

Serves 4-6

INGREDIENTS
2 × 15-ounce cans lychees
1 fresh mango *or* 15-ounce can
   sliced mangoes
2 tbsps cornstarch
Finely grated zest of 1 lemon
2 tbsps lemon juice
⅔ cup heavy cream
A few drops of yellow food
   coloring (optional)
1 tbsp ground almonds
Toasted flaked almonds to
   decorate (optional)

Drain the lychees and the
mangoes and reserve ¾ cup
lychee and ½ cup mango syrup.
Mix the syrups together and keep
to one side. If using fresh mango,
reserve all the juice from the
lychees and make up to 1¼ cups
by adding cold water. Place the
cornstarch in a pan and add a
little syrup to make a smooth
paste. Gradually add the rest of

the syrup and mix thoroughly.
Add the lemon zest and juice and
cook over low heat until the
mixture boils and thickens. Let
cool.

Beat the cream until thick, then
stir it into the cornstarch mixture
with the food coloring (if used).
Add the ground almonds and
mix well. Remove any broken
lychees, chop them finely and
add them to the cornstarch
mixture. Reserve the whole
lychees. Chop the mango slices
roughly.

Stuff each whole lychee with
chopped mangoes so that the
mango is about ¼ inch higher
than the top of each lychee. Add
any remaining mango pieces or
pulp to the cornstarch mixture.
Line a 10-inch pie plate with the
cornstarch mixture and arrange
the lychees on top (the
cornstarch mixture will line a
smaller dish rather too thickly
and the lychees will sink).
Decorate with flaked almonds if
wished. Chill before serving.

WHEAT FUDGE

Use a very fine whole wheat flour for this recipe – a bread flour simply will not work as it contains too much coarse bran. Chapati flour is ideal.

Serves 10-12

INGREDIENTS
½ cup ghee or sweet butter
2 cups fine textured whole wheat
   flour
1½ tsps ground cardamom seeds
2 tbsps broken nut meats
½ cup light brown sugar

Melt the ghee in a pan over medium heat and add the flour, stir and mix thoroughly. Cook for 5 minutes, stirring continuously. Turn the heat down and cook for a further 10-12 minutes, stirring continuously. Add the cardamom and broken nuts, stir and cook for 2-3 minutes, then remove from the heat and add the sugar. Mix well, and if there are any lumps, break them up with the back of the spoon.

Lightly grease a large plate and spread the flour mixture on it. Using the back of a metal spoon, spread the mixture evenly to form a large square, about ½ inch thick, 6 inches wide and 8 inches long. Let the mixture cool, then chill for 20 minutes. Remove from the refrigerator and cut into 1½-2 inch squares. Let the fudge harden before serving. Store in an open container or plate in the refrigerator. The fudge will keep for 3-4 weeks.

JEERA PANI

Cumin has always been noted for its ability to aid digestion – this is cumin water, a good appetizer to serve before a heavy meal.

Serves 4

INGREDIENTS
2 tbsps cumin seeds
2½ cups water
2-3 dried red chilies
1 tbsp freshly chopped mint
    leaves *or* 1 tsp dried mint
1 tsp salt
1 tsp sugar
1 tbsp lemon juice

Heat a cast iron, or heavy based pan and dry-roast the cumin seeds until they are a shade darker. Crush them lightly in a pestle and mortar. Bring the water to a boil in a pan. Add the cumin, chilies, mint, salt and sugar, then cover the pan and simmer for 15 minutes. Stir in the lemon juice, then remove the pan from the heat. Let the drink cool, then strain it into individual glasses.

SPICY PINEAPPLE PUNCH

Pineapples are a traditional symbol of hospitality – this is an excellent drink with which to greet your friends.

Serves 6-8

INGREDIENTS
2 cups water
4½ cups pineapple juice
5 cinnamon sticks, 2 inches long, broken up
12 whole cloves
12 green cardamoms, bruised
1 tbsp freshly chopped mint leaves
¾ cup brandy

Place the water, half the pineapple juice, and the cinnamon, cloves, lightly crushed cardamom and mint in a pan. Bring to a boil, cover the pan and simmer gently for 20 minutes. Remove from the heat and let cool, keeping the pan covered. Strain the drink and add the remaining pineapple juice and the brandy. Mix well and chill before serving.

NIMBU PANI

This is a spicy refreshing drink for hot weather.

Serves 4

INGREDIENTS
2 tbsps superfine sugar
1 tsp salt
2½ cups water
Juice of 1 lemon
Crushed ice
4 slices of lemon

Place the sugar and salt in the water and stir until dissolved, then stir in the lemon juice. Place the crushed ice in individual glasses and strain the nimbu pani into the glasses over the ice. Top with the sliced lemon and serve.

MANGO SHERBET

This recipe makes a thick sherbert drink with the luxurious flavor of mango. Thin it with more milk if preferred, or top with a scoop of vanilla ice cream.

Serves 4-6

INGREDIENTS

2 × 15-ounce cans of sliced
  mangoes, drained
2½ cups milk
4 tbsps superfine sugar
1 tsp ground cardamom seeds
1 tbsp rosewater (optional)
1¼ cups cold water

Place the mango slices, half the milk, the sugar, cardamom and rosewater in a blender or food processor and mix for a few seconds. Transfer the contents to a large jug or bowl and add the remaining milk and the water. Chill for 2-3 hours before serving.

RASAM

This is a hot drink flavored with lentils and seasoned with spiced oil.

Serves 4-6

INGREDIENTS
4 cups water
¼ cup masoor dhal (red split
  lentils), washed and drained
1 tsp coriander seeds
1 tsp cumin seeds
2 dried red chilies
6-8 curry leaves
1 level tsp tamarind concentrate
  or 1 tbsp lemon juice
1 tsp salt
1 tsp paprika
1 tbsp cooking oil
½ tsp black mustard seeds

Place the water, dhal, coriander, cumin, chilies and curry leaves in a pan and bring to a boil.

Lower the heat to medium and cook, uncovered, for 6-8 minutes. Cover the pan and simmer for 30 minutes. Remove the pan from the heat and let cool slightly. Strain the liquid and sieve the dhal into it. Return it to the pan. Heat and add the tamarind or lemon juice, salt and paprika. Stir until the tamarind is dissolved.

Heat the oil in a separate pan and add the mustard seeds. As soon as the seeds crackle, add the rasam or stir the hot oil and the seeds into the rasam. Remove from heat and serve warm.

SPICED TEA

Spiced or flavored teas have long been popular drinks in India – I use Assam tea in this recipe.

Serves 2

INGREDIENTS
2 cups water
6 whole cloves
6 green cardamoms
1 cinnamon stick, 2 inches long,
  broken up
3 tsps tea leaves or 2 tea bags
Milk and sugar to taste

Place the water in a pan and bring to a boil. Lightly crush the cardamoms. Add the spices, cover the pan and simmer for 10 minutes. Rinse a teapot with hot water and add the tea leaves or the tea bags. Bring the spiced liquid to a boil again and strain it into the teapot. Brew for 5 minutes and serve with milk and sugar to taste.

INDEX